TIME SONG

TIME SONG

Journeys in Search of a
Submerged Land

Julia Blackburn

with drawings by Enrique Brinkmann

PANTHEON BOOKS
NEW YORK

All rights reserved. Published in the United States by Pantheon Books, a division of Penguin Random House LLC, New York. Originally published in hardcover in Great Britain by Jonathan Cape, an imprint of Vintage Publishing, a division of Penguin Random House Ltd., London, in 2019.

Pantheon Books and colophon are registered trademarks of Penguin Random House LLC.

Grateful acknowledgment is made to David Higham Associates for permission to reprint an excerpt from "Eden Rock," by Charles Causley, from *Collected Poems, 1951–2000* by Charles Causley (London: Picador, 2000). Copyright © 2000 by the Estate of Charles Causley. Reprinted by permission of David Higham Associates.

Library of Congress Cataloging-in-Publication Data
Names: Blackburn, Julia, author. Brinkmann, Enrique, illustrator.
Title: Time song : Journeys in search of a submerged land /
Julia Blackburn ; illustrated by Enrique Brinkmann.
Description: First United States edition. New York : Pantheon Books, 2019.
Includes bibliographical references and index.
Identifiers: LCCN 2018048745. ISBN 9781101871676
(hardcover : alk. paper). ISBN 9781101871683 (ebook).
Subjects: LCSH: North Sea Region—Description and travel. North Sea Region—Antiquities. Submerged lands—North Sea Region—History. Prehistoric peoples—North Sea Region. Mesolithic period—North Sea Region. Blackburn, Julia—Travel—North Sea Region. England—Description and travel. Europe, Northern—Description and travel.
Classification: LCC D965.5 .B55 2019 | DDC 909/.096336—dc23 |
LC record available at https://lccn.loc.gov/2018048745

www.pantheonbooks.com

Jacket art: "Los Mesoliticos XI" by Enrique Brinkmann © 2019
Artists Rights Society (ARS), New York / VEGAP, Madrid
Jacket design by Jenny Carrow

Printed in the United States of America
First United States Edition
2 4 6 8 9 7 5 3 1

A great while ago, the world begun,
With hey, ho, the wind and the rain . . .

SHAKESPEARE, *Twelfth Night*

'OH,' I SAY CASUALLY, as if in answer to a question, 'I'm writing about a country called Doggerland. It's also known as North Sea Land because that's where it was, under what is now the North Sea. It emerged after the last Ice Age and with the warming of the climate it became a wonderfully fertile place of rivers and lakes, gently rounded hills and sheltered valleys, reed beds and salt marshes in the lowlands, trees on higher ground and a profusion of life: fish, birds, animals and humans as well. These were a people who left few traces of their passing. They hunted with weapons made from wood, bone or stone; they had canoes cut from the trunks of trees; they had dogs working with them and sometimes buried their dead alongside their dogs. But as the ice went on melting the sea levels rose dramatically – you can't believe how fast, it could be more than two metres within a century – so the land was inundated, familiar places submerged or made inaccessible. Seven thousand years ago, Doggerbank was still there as an island and then it too was gone.

'And,' I continue, carried forward by the idea of it all, 'I am also writing about what happened in this same area long before the last Ice Age. I go back to the first humans who were here, close to where I live: a cache of worked flints was found quite recently near a holiday camp and then a bit further up the coast there is the little flurry of footsteps fossilised in what was once the soft mud of a river estuary. Five people pottering about some nine hundred thousand years ago; they were probably collecting plants and shellfish.

'Mammoth,' I say, 'great herds of them moving across the grassy steppes when Britain was part of the Eurasian land mass. I've collected quite a lot of mammoth bones, along with those of other extinct creatures; it's best to go looking after a storm has scoured the edges of the cliffs to reveal whatever secrets they have been hiding, but I often forget to go then. I did pick up a lovely stone axehead just recently. It looks like nothing much until you hold it in your hand and feel how well it fits, how sharp it is.

'Of course I ask myself what on earth I think I'm doing, rattling around like a ghost in such distant landscapes of the past, and this is what might be the answer, or at least part of the answer. I am not especially afraid of my own death, but I am afraid of the death of forests and oceans, the contamination of water and air, the sense that we are heading towards a catastrophe from which there will be no escape. I comfort myself with the knowledge that this is nothing new: the climate has often shifted from extremes of heat to extremes of cold; oceans rising to cover the land and shrinking to reveal it in a different form; living creatures emerging in all their strangeness and determination to survive and some of them manage to hold on, but others do not.

'I wonder now if it makes more sense to imagine infinity going backwards in time, rather than forwards. When you look at it that way round, you no longer have the vague dread of what the future holds, instead there is the intimation of the enormity of everything that has gone before: a solemn procession of life in all its myriad forms moving steadily towards this present moment. You can almost hear the songs they are singing.

'There is something else. My husband died a few years ago. He has vanished and yet he remains close, beneath the surface as it were, so perhaps I am also trying to catch a glimpse of him within the great jumble of everything else that has been lost from our sight.'

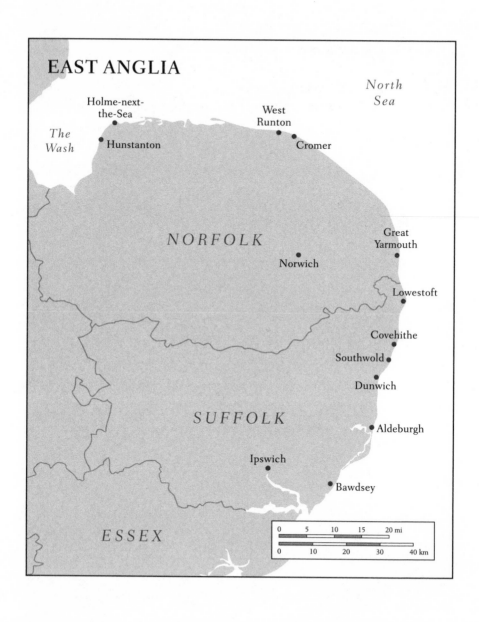

EAST ANGLIA

*North
Sea*

*The
Wash*

Holme-next-
the-Sea
Hunstanton

West
Runton
Cromer

NORFOLK

Norwich

Great
Yarmouth

Lowestoft

Covehithe
Southwold
Dunwich

SUFFOLK

Aldeburgh

Ipswich

Bawdsey

ESSEX

0	5	10	15	20 mi
0	10	20	30	40 km

CONTENTS

Part One

Old Time

They beckon to me from the other bank.
I hear them call, 'See where the stream-path is!
Crossing is not as hard as you might think!'

I had not thought that it would be like this.

CHARLES CAUSLEY, 'Eden Rock'

1

I am looking out across the North Sea on a calm day. The surface of the sea is like a covering of grey skin, breathing softly in and out.

As I stand here, the water that separates me from the mainland on the other side begins to retreat, as if a plug has been pulled. A vast country emerges: low hills and wide valleys, the twist and turn of rivers, the scoop of lakes.

At first this country appears limp and without colour, but then a shiver of life moves through it. The birds flying overhead spiral down to settle and pause on their journey. Seeds take root. Reed beds and salt marshes spread out like shadows across the young mud. Tiny trees appear on higher ground. The rivers are again flowing and fish are racing down them towards a more distant ocean. The old lakes are filling up and animals are moving in, exploring the territory; humans, too, since this is a human time.

I fail to catch the moment of the change taking place, but now the sea is rising. Peninsulas become islands, islands disappear without trace, rivers break through the banks that defined them. The lower lands are flooded and even before they fall, the trees on higher ground are killed by the salt water in which they stand. The animals and the humans must escape if they are to survive. For a while the marshes and reed beds remain, but then they go under.

I am on a beach close to the shoreline and looking out across the breathing surface of the North Sea. Slabs of thick, peaty soil containing the roots and broken stalks of those reeds from long ago lie scattered on the sand. I pick up a piece of mammoth bone, brown and heavy and still showing the honeycomb that once carried blood and lymph through the living body. I pick up a shell that has been turned into a stone. I look for flints worked into the shape of a weapon or a tool.

It's getting late. I go home.

2

I live close to the sea and the sea I live close to covers a country we now call Doggerland. This country has been through many incarnations: hot and dry, wet and marshy, cold and ice-bound, but for most of its long time it has in one way or another connected England with mainland Europe.

Much of the fragmented evidence of what this country once was is hidden under the sea, but there is also a lot to be found scattered in the sands and clays and gravels of the land. Deep time lies beneath my feet and if I were to dig into the earth I would witness the past unfolding in layers.

The coastline here is delicate and unprotected; a storm can easily break off great chunks of the soft cliff to reveal lines of brightly coloured sands, a string of dancing shells followed by a band of gravel and then of clay. Bones as well. Just a few weeks ago I found a fossilised piece from the jigsaw of an ancient sea creature, lying below a field where carrots were being harvested, and once I found a human skull, packed tight with soil in which the roots of little plants were growing.

I have been gathering these broken treasures for many years and as I look at them, or rearrange them in different configurations, they seem to become part of my own thought process, part of who I am.

There is a pond in the meadow behind this house. When I first saw it the pond was nothing but mud and the broken skeletons of dead trees and during a particularly dry summer I managed to fish out an enamel teapot and an unbroken Victorian ink bottle with that nice creamy pottery glaze. Now the pond is deep and clean, marsh marigolds around its edges and a family of moorhens scattering across its surface. The tall sycamore tree close by has an odd bend in its trunk caused by its proximity to the brick chimney which was for a while the last remaining evidence of an old farmhouse.

Do you understand? I'm doing practice work here: looking at the tree and seeing the absent chimney, looking at the pond and seeing the wreck of mud. And then I take another step back and the tree has not yet started to grow and the pond is filled with a wriggling mass of tadpoles, from the days when frogs and toads were plentiful in this part of the world. I try to catch a glimpse of the grey silhouette of the cuckoo that no longer comes here to announce the return of spring. I listen to the silence and populate it with the hesitant ding-dong of the cuckoo's voice.

I walk a bit further to what is called Castle Meadow: a perfect circle surrounded by oak trees and defined by a ditch that floods in the winter. I allow the simple image of a castle to take shape like a child's drawing and I can see horses pulling carts, dogs following behind, people going through a gate, but then I am distracted and they vanish.

I go to the field that we called the butterfly meadow because in the summer a mass of little butterflies, meadow blues mostly, would billow out in clouds of soft pastel colours as you moved through the tangle of purple flowering vetch that grew among the grasses, and as the butterflies danced I always pictured the children of long ago dancing among them. Perhaps they were on their way to scare crows or pick up flints and set them in heaps. Perhaps they were barefoot. The meadow has become a wheat field and the butterflies have gone.

And then to the adjacent field where I used to find so many fossils, in the days when the farmer who died was still alive. This was the grumpy farmer who went to Australia after a scandal with a local girl, he whose father was made to live in the chicken house at the end of the garden because his mother had banished him there and the grumpy farmer brought food on a plate to his banished father and I suppose that was where his anger started. He never allowed modern machinery on his land and so the ploughing didn't damage the fossil field. Over the years I found dozens of stone sea creatures in the heavy clay soil, *loving soil* they called it because it clung to your boots so fiercely you could hardly lift one foot and then the other, and as I walked through that field, I would turn it in my mind into a shallow sea.

Yesterday I went, as I often do, to the nearby village of Covehithe. It has an eighteenth-century church standing within the ruins of a much older church. A narrow road passes the church and heads straight for the sea, but it has no final destination because it has snapped off like a piece of biscuit right at the cliff edge: a layer of tarmac and concrete sticking out over the drop beneath, changing shape after each new succession of high tides.

I followed the path from the village to the coast. Gulls were dipping and holding themselves steady in the air as if they had little hooks in their backs attached to elasticated strings. A kestrel: a glint of tawny feathers. The last of the sand martins.

I slept for one night on the sand of this beach with my first husband beside me and our second child stirring in my belly. We lay on a duvet and under a duvet and I remember the slowness of the sunset and geese creaking and crying in long skeins above our heads. The noise of them stepped over into my dreams.

It must have been around the same time I saw two friends entering the shallow sea hand in hand and laughing and it had never occurred to me before that they were also young in their way, even though they were already as old as I am now. She had recently been treated for a cancer which almost killed her and in order to pull herself through the process of recovery she started to build a flint wall in her garden and every day she went to the beach and chose a big flint and carried it to the car and brought it back and cemented it in place and slowly her strength returned to her as the wall grew.

Once I noticed a tiny black thing as hard and shiny as polished jet, tightly embedded in the sand of the cliff. I pulled it out like a thorn and it appeared to be a fossilised chrysalis. I could see the tightly folded wings and little circles under which lay the still-closed eyes of a creature that never got round to splitting out of its prison and emerging as a moth or a butterfly.

I found my first piece of mammoth here: an almost complete section of vertebra. I keep it on a window ledge, next to a beautiful stone axe from this same beach and another one which my son, who was stirring in my womb while I listened to the geese, picked up a little while ago in the mud of the Thames, close to Tate Modern. There have been so many Thames Picks, as they are called, found along that stretch of the river that people think they were not lost accidentally, but were offerings to whatever gods were interested in such gifts.

Yesterday the coast looked very battered. Big pieces of land had tumbled down, some of them tufty-topped with fresh grass or with the Chinese lantern shapes of a recent sugar beet crop. Within the side of the wounded cliff I could see the arterial systems of drainage pipes and rolls of barbed wire from the defences of the last war or the war before that one. Things here often appear magically out of nowhere and then vanish with an equal magic. Recently a concrete pillbox settled its awkward weight on the sand like a prehistoric creature, and it reminded me of the last scene in *Planet of the Apes* when Charlton Heston thinks he is back in the dawn of time but then he sees the arm of the Statue of Liberty sticking up out of the sand, along with the spiked crown and the 1920s haircut, and he realises he has arrived in the future and the sand is covering the city of New York.

A friend told me of the nuclear command bunker which lies under the lawn of a garden in the village. Everything is hearsay but it seems it was built during the Cold War and is connected to its twin on the Dutch coast. It is three storeys deep, with enough room to hold thirty important people and enough dry and tinned food to feed them for thirty years. He took a series of photographs inside the bunker with an infrared camera. One of them shows a dour 1960s domestic interior in which a bulbous television set stands close to two stiff armchairs upholstered in that plastic material called leatherette. Another is of a printed notice on a wall with practical information about what you must and must not do, next to a very amateur oil painting of the church and a pinkly flowering cherry tree, all of it set against the bright blue of a summer sky, so the underground people need never forget the look of the world they had lost.

I keep thinking of the bunker and how every year it is being brought closer and closer to the cliff edge, until the day comes when it will begin to topple down on to the beach and maybe strangers with no idea of what it once was will stare at the debris and take away anything they consider worth saving.

3

In 1946 a sparrowhawk flew into the French windows of my great-aunt's house. Molly, she was called, and she had been dressed in the black of deepest mourning ever since the death of her younger sister, an event she considered her fault because she had said it would not rain, but it did rain and the sister caught a cold which became the pneumonia that killed her.

The sparrowhawk was only stunned, but a week later it made the same dive into the glittering firmament of glass and that was the end of it. My great-aunt had the bird stuffed and mounted very simply on a white perch set in a white box, with an account of what had happened written on a label glued to the back of the box.

I saw the hawk on the day I first met my great-aunt. She was in her eighties and I had just turned five. She was in the hall to welcome us and I looked up and there it was looking down at me with a quizzical gaze. She noticed this encounter and told me how the bird had died and I must have been a good listener because when her story was finished she said I could have it; I could take it with me when my holiday came to an end. And so I did. The glass case sat next to me like a new friend on the back seat of my parents' black Ford Popular, all the way from Northumberland to London.

It has been with me ever since, accompanying me through my life. I've transported its fragile bulk from place to place, setting it up in one room or another, the feet grasping tightly on the perch, the head tilted and alert, and as our eyes met I'd feel reassured that we were both much the same as we always had been. It's here now on top of a bookcase. Time and direct sunlight have caused the delicate brown markings on its feathers to fade into a uniformity of dusty white and mouse grey, just as my hair has faded and lost its colour.

After the sparrowhawk and still young – a solitary child given to observing rather than talking – I became the owner of the jaw of a fox, the teeth sharp and dangerous and ready to bite; the skull of a ram from whose white forehead the twisting horns erupted with an energy that seemed to me miraculous; a single deer antler, the skin of a marmot, the shell of a tortoise and the desiccated body of a toad given to me with uncharacteristic ceremony by my maternal grandmother. For a while I had a bushbaby as a pet, a gentle creature who perched under the jungle leaves of my hair and held on to my ear as we spent the evenings together. When it died suddenly and unexpectedly, I buried the little body in a metal tin that had held powdered milk and, in a very matter-of-fact manner, I dug it up some months later, the skeleton white and clean, the huge eye sockets staring at me with the recollection of limpid brown eyes.

Everything speaks of what it has been: the leg bone of a wading bird holds the image of that bird standing on the mud of a shoreline, poised on its own mirror reflection. The almost weightless skull of an owl which I found when I first came here allows me to see one of its kind drifting silently in the dusk, quartering the meadows that surround this garden, and my husband is beside me and we watch it together, even though as I walk away he remains by the gate where we stood on that particular evening.

There was a pale and almost transparent moon in the sky this morning. The air has become very autumnal. It will soon be my husband's second death year but because of the strange mathematics of absence, his age no longer increases with the passing of time. At night I sometimes stretch out my hand towards him and wait until I am almost convinced that an answering hand is there, even though I cannot feel it. I'm sure this is quite usual. It's what people do.

Time Song 1

I am sixty-seven,
already quite a long while
to be here in the world.
My husband who died
was eleven years older than me:
war spreading across Europe
and as a child he saw people assembled in the square
near where he lived,
his best friend taken away
never to return.

Both my grandmothers
were born in the 1880s.
One gave me a flat, white object,
a fusion of bone and stone
which she said was a tiger's paw,
but I know it's a piece of mammoth tooth.
I have a few photographs of her
and other stiff-backed family members,
most of whom I never met;
they hold still while the camera shutter
traps their image on sensitive paper.

My parents are dead.
I have kept some of their things
as an aspect of memory.
I have a vivid recollection of my father
and if I want to
I can seem to hear his speaking voice.
My mother is more absent
except in dreams.

My two granddaughters are still young;
they walk with precarious confidence
and babble words that are not yet words.
I look at their faces which hold the secret
of who they already are
and who they are becoming.
I find it strangely reassuring to think
— if all goes well —
they will be alive for a long time
after I am dead.

According to a little book I have owned for ages,
the earth was born four thousand five hundred million years ago
at the start of the Cryptozoic Eon.
The most ancient rocks can be dated
at three thousand eight hundred million years,
but I have no idea what was happening during the interim.

Algal reefs were defining the oceans
two thousand million years ago,
and then came green algae and soft-bodied animals.
The Palaeozoic began with shellfish,
five hundred and seventy million years ago.

Vertebrates, plants and amphibia followed,
Until the jump-back is two hundred and twenty-five million years
and the Mesozoic is beginning
and here are the great reptiles of the Triassic, the Jurassic and
    the Cretaceous.

The Cainzoic
– and I must look up its meaning;
it would be odd if it relates to the man
who killed his brother
with the jawbone of an ass –
started sixty-five million years ago
and encompassed the mammals,
as the Eocene became the Oligocene,
the Miocene and the Pliocene.

During the last two million years of the Pleistocene
which has been and gone
and the Holocene where we more or less still are,
humans took shape:
Homo ergaster, erectus, heidelbergensis
and *sapiens* which is us;

all balancing that big skull,
eyes set forward,
dexterous fingers
good at holding tight
and making things.

Based on the diagram in a book called *Rocks* by David Dineley, published in 1976 as part of the Collins Countryside Series, 'intended to offer the beginner a modern introduction to British natural history'. I know it's out of date, but never mind, it tells the gist of the story.

4

Ages ago and only for a few months, I was living with a rather drunken American writer called Mason. He was very preoccupied with linear time, which he declared was an artificial construct that hemmed us in and was the cause of much of our impatience and sense of inadequacy. 'We got to get rid of it!' he said in his loud New York bark and, eager young thing that I was, I tried to do just that. Sometimes and much to my surprise, it worked for a few fleeting seconds and then it was as if past, present and future no longer existed, leaving me dizzy from the exhilaration that came with the loss.

I have always kept some sort of record of what was happening in my life. I started with diaries as a teenager and when I found it difficult to put my troubles into words I made drawings instead. Aged twenty-five and living in Amsterdam, I met the man who would be my first husband and to chronicle this new trajectory I stripped an old family photograph album of all my remote, dour ancestors – their cars and houses, their horses and dogs – replacing them with labels from tins of food I'd bought in the Chinese supermarket in the Red Light District. Bean curd from Hong Kong, salt lettuce from Thailand, salted goose from China and fried fish from I don't know where, but the smiling fish is swimming in a beautiful blue sea the same colour as itself. Now when I look at the album I read it as a story of romance and adventure, while knowing that each label also represents aspects of the past that I was throwing away.

Later, pregnant with my second child and living on a farm in Suffolk, I began making a casual inventory of what I was thinking and seeing and dreaming. I had just got hold of a copy of a wonderful nineteenth-century account of the stories and beliefs of the |Xam Bushmen, hunter-gatherers who inhabited a world in which humans lived in a sort of eternal present moment and saw themselves as one animal among many with no sense of dominion. The book impressed me more than anything I had ever read.

I was in southern Spain in 2001, visiting the house where the painter Goya had stayed just after the illness which left him stone deaf. I found myself watching dung beetles scurrying around the roots of a carob tree with the peculiar self-absorption of their tribe, and there was Goya also watching these same beetles that briefly allowed him to forget the isolating disaster of his deafness.

5

It's seven thirty in the morning and I am sitting in bed with a cup of tea. The autumn light is golden in the garden and I am reading about the Eocene, which lasted from fifty-six to just under thirty-four million years ago. The Greek name means *New Dawn,* because so many new creatures appeared under its watch as it were, although a lot of the old ones disappeared as well, thanks to an event called La Grande Coupure: The Big Cut or Snip.

This is all because yesterday I went to East Lane in the village of Bawdsey and I am trying to piece together what it is and what it was; alongside what I saw and what I did not and could not see. I brought

18

back a few bits of fossilised wood, from a mangrove swamp most probably, as well as something which looks as if it might be a seed head, but I have no means of identifying what sort of plant it once belonged to. Like a sombre variation of the transforming touch of King Midas, everything I found that was once organic has been turned into iron, thanks to a combination of iron pyrites in the mud and some chemical process caused by a lack of oxygen. These transmuted objects lie about, scattered in casual drifts in the soft cracks and rivulets of a bed of London Clay which itself is a remnant of the Eocene. As well as being heavy and looking at first glance like shrapnel from a recent war, they – the objects – also look exactly like what they once were: branch and twig, fruit and pod, perfectly true to their original form and yet sinister in their oddness.

The clay in which they lie was originally grey and brown silt, carried down to what was then a different sea by big sluggish rivers. This was in the middle Eocene and the earth, having got very hot and steamy with little or no ice anywhere, not even at the two poles, was cooling again, thanks in part to something called the Azolla Event; the azolla being a floating aquatic fern which apparently flourished extraordinarily well in the Arctic Ocean and then sank in great rotting heaps to the bottom, where it absorbed the excess production of carbon dioxide in the atmosphere and thus changed the climate.

A second cup of tea. One of my two chickens was killed by a friend's friendly dog just a couple of days ago. It was alive when I picked it up after the shock of the attack and then the eyes flickered and the life went out as if a switch had been turned. I kept a couple of the pretty feathers as a memento and buried everything else in the top part of the garden. I can now hear the other chicken, which seems to have hardly noticed the loss; it is standing outside the French windows and making elongated burbling noises, to express a hunger for breakfast. I ignore it and persist with the Eocene for a while. I make lots of pencil notes in my notebook because otherwise I could never hold so much surreal information.

There I was at Bawdsey, parked just behind a sea wall and next to a curious compound closed off by a high wire fence, behind which stood a collection of diggers and earth movers, looking like creatures in a zoo, or perhaps a natural history museum is more accurate, since they were fixed in lifeless poses. I was with my friend Helena who studied Classics at Cambridge and has a wonderful breathing bellow of a laugh that always surprises me because it doesn't sound as if it could be made by a human being.

We walked the narrow path that runs across the top of the sea wall, past a couple of quite prim houses and a Martello tower, built as one of one hundred and three such structures to protect these shores from Napoleon's invading army which never came. The tower has an incongruous chimney on its roof and a wooden staircase leading up to a high front door, but the staircase looked very unsafe and the people who lived here have clearly gone somewhere else.

And then we were flanked by a heaped-up display of big square-cut stone boulders imported from Denmark I think it was, or maybe Norway. They are supposed to hold the sea back and keep the land safe, but they seemed a bit nonchalant and not very convincing in their sense of purpose. Beyond them we came to a first sight of the sweep of coastline that was my destination, the focus of my study: a delicate scooped-out, half-moon-shaped bay, backed by a rather tatty cliff, with tiered banks of steep shingle in front of it. Below the line of the shingle lay the wide expanse of muddy clay which is revealed with each low tide and during the summer months is much covered by a bright green weed which I believe is called Mermaid's Hair, but maybe that was just what I called it when I was a child.

The clay stretched out, as flat as a football pitch. It was littered with a collection of lopsided boxes which I knew were part of later military defences, erected during the First and Second World Wars to protect these shores from invading Germans and their tanks and weaponry. From a distance they made me think of pieces from an abandoned board game.

We followed the increasingly narrow path which could have been made by rabbits. Larks flew up in sudden flurries. There were lots of them. Now we were stepping on to the noisy shingle and almost at once, among an accumulation of whelk shells turned chalk white by time and the weather, we were confronted by a beautiful dead gannet, its neck stretched out as if still in flight. The eyes were black and empty and, unlike my chicken's, they had remained open.

We went down to the edge of the clay. Helena found it too slippery and kept to the shingle, while I pottered about in the familiar bent-over posture that I adopt whenever I am on a beach or a ploughed field that seems to hold the chance of finding treasure. I picked things up, surprised each time by the metallic weight of them. I discarded some and kept others to rattle in my pocket. I was in that nice abstraction in which nothing exists in all the world beyond the walls of a concentrated gaze. Small thoughts, but not many of them. The skin of my hands began to absorb a metallic stink.

In the new dawn of the Eocene when these fossils were still vivid with their own life, a warm sea covered much of south-east England.

It was up to one hundred metres deep and it was fed by rivers which, as well as the clay sediment, also carried the flotsam and jetsam of plant debris, logs and branches. The climate was sub-tropical and the land flourished with a mass of luxuriant rainforests: monkey puzzles, six varieties of palm, members of the avocado and cinnamon family, mulberry, fig, walnut and pecan, waterlily and fern, as well as Norfolk pine and witchhazel. A barricade of thick mangrove swamps straddled the mud all along the coast. In the bright, cold, autumnal air, I tried to snatch a glimpse of what once was.

Shark and ray and turtles and all sorts of fish and crustaceans inhabited the salt water, while other turtles and big relatives of the crocodile and the alligator were in the waters where the rivers approached the sea. In the forests you might see the *pantodont,* which was a sort of elephant, an early variety of horse no bigger than a roe deer and, nesting in the trees, a species of owl, along with parrots and other birds.

What I found so odd in being there on Bawdsey beach was the merging of the very ancient past with the very recent past and the way they seemed to be caught up in an intimate conversation with each other, their voices overlapping. The tilting and broken carapaces of pillboxes were like the exoskeletons of enormous crabs or dwellings made by a species of hominid that left only this trace of its passing. The seawater sloshed at their walls, the pyrite fossils nestled at their edges, and limpets were almost indistinguishable from the pebble-dash excrescences of reinforced concrete.

Further along, there were things known as dragon's teeth: angled iron stakes, laced with barbed wire and installed to stop men from struggling to land once their boats had brought them close enough, or to tear them to pieces if they couldn't resist the carrying force of the waves. Such sharp teeth could just as well have been the defensive broken branches from the mangrove swamps guarding the shore of a tropical sea against invasion. Beyond the line of the dragon's teeth I came across a scattering of anti-tank blocks resembling huge vertebrae, from a *crocodylid* perhaps, or an *alligatoroid*.

Five o'clock and Helena had grown tired and was sitting and staring at the horizon. The air was humid and warm and the sun was beginning to sink. I went on for a couple of hundred yards or so, until I was walking beneath some sort of military installation built on the cliff above, with rather menacing street lights planted close to the edge. I turned back, following the base of the cliff. I found some nice shells, ancient bivalves stained a dark yellow ochre, and again that curious confusion in which old things appeared to be bright and new, while scraps of expanded polystyrene and other modern rubbish were masquerading as survivors from another age.

And so we returned to the car park and drove away. We followed a different route, along narrow roads flanked by high hedges, and at one stage we were driving through the outskirts of a prison complex and there were several rather mysterious road signs telling us to THINK KEYS. By now the sky was streaked a fierce orange, as if dipped in a bath of molten metal.

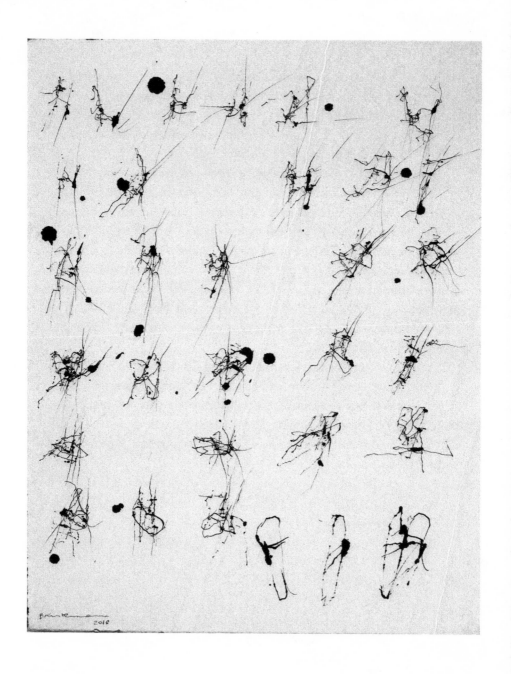

Time Song 2

Fifty-five to thirty-five million years ago,
when the clays, sands and gravels
of the London and Hampshire basins
were being laid down in shallow seas,
birds in Britain became more plentiful,
their forms close
to what we know today.

The line of evidence was broken
by ice and time
until some two million years ago,
and here come eagle owls and snowy owls,
large auks since vanished;
and the North Atlantic albatross,
found in the Red Crag of Suffolk,
also gone.

During the coldest periods
of the Pleistocene
sea levels fell one hundred metres,
revealing an expanse of land
not wholly obscured by ice:

dry and vegetated,
forested in places,
with small lakes and swamps,
good for Arctic water fowl
among others.

The bodies of birds
that died in the open
tended to be destroyed
by predators or scavengers,
but a few bones have survived
in the sands, gravels and clays
from rivers, swamps and lakes,
while the remains of owls and rock doves,
swifts and swallows,
starlings, jackdaws and red-billed choughs
have been found,
embedded in the thin layers of soil and debris
on cave floors.

Other birds which did not live in caves
but were carried in to be eaten,
might leave a scattering of feathers
or fragments of bone:
delicate relics
of their passing.

The Cromer Forest Beds
hold the story of birds
from around a million years ago;
the summers were a bit warmer then:
fresh water in fens and rivers,
open grassy areas,
mixed woodlands,
and, among the trees,
blackbird and ring ouzel,
song thrush and redwing,
nuthatch,
starling and jay.

Based on *The History of the Birds of Britain* by Colin Harrison, Collins, 1988. In the preface the author says, 'I have tried to put the birds of Britain into their long-term context. All too often we look at them as though they were a mainly twentieth-century invention, with a few honoured by a passing mention in our written history. In fact, although we only see them within our own brief span of time, they are an assemblage of species that in slightly varying combinations has existed within a continuity stretching back at least a couple of million years.'

6

I made a visit to Jerusalem in 1996. It was before the first Intifada, although things already seemed to have reached breaking point. I was there with a friend and we were staying on the Palestinian side of the city and people kept thinking I was a Palestinian returning to my homeland after a long absence and I liked that for the sense it gave me of belonging in a country I did not know.

One day we went exploring among the back streets and came to a rectangular pool of water cut into the fleshy white marble on which Jerusalem is built and the pool was fed by a spring carried in a carved trough that came out of a tunnel.

A man came up to us and said, 'Do you want to see where Jesus performed the miracle of the blind man?' and we both said yes, because of course we did. 'Take off your shoes and trousers,' he said to my friend. 'Take off your shoes and roll up your skirt,' he said to me and we were instantly obedient, partly from surprise.

He led the way into the tunnel, our bare feet treading on the side of the watercourse. The wall was rounded and smooth, cold to the touch. We walked into complete darkness, our eyes irrelevant, only the feel of the hand on the stone to guide us. And then all at once the shape of the wall changed as it formed a soft scoop, big enough for the three of us to stand in a group instead of a line. 'Turn around!' said our guide. 'Here the blind man could see!' We turned and in the far distance there was a tiny pinpoint of light which was the mouth of the tunnel and that was the miracle.

*

Back to February 2015 and a young man called Jonathan found the jaw of a rhinoceros embedded in the hard mud of the Cromer Forest Bed. This stretch of the bed is just a two-minute walk from the beach car park in West Runton and the tea shop where you can buy plastic buckets and spades and seriously sweet cake and strong tea and you can look at a laminated sheet of paper which tells the story of the discovery of the almost complete skeleton of a mammoth, who stood four metres tall at his shoulder and was twice as heavy as a mature bull elephant. That was in 1999 and most of the mammoth is now on display in the local museum although a section of it was too difficult to dig up and still lies in its original grave, covered by a slab of concrete to stop fossil hunters trying to get hold of a few more bones. Other laminated sheets explain a lot about how flint and chalk are formed and why this particular area is so important for what it holds of the past.

The freshwater beds are the remaining scraps of the muddy banks of an ancient and extinct river from the days when the sea was land and the land was thick with all sorts of life. The evidence of the continuation of this river's journey now lies under the sand of the beach and stretches out for some distance beneath the sea's surface. Where the sea has not yet encroached, patches of the river bank survive as a cliff of very dense clay, some forty metres in length and reaching to a height of around three metres. The clay is heaped up in smooth mounds like sleeping beasts and it looks as though it might have been dumped there by a builder's merchant, until you notice the white scraps from broken shells, marking the lines of time passing.

Jonathan knows how to find fossils. It's as if he sees them in the darkness where they lie hidden, as if they call out to him in a voice that only he can hear. He goes in search of them very regularly, every day if the weather has been rough. One late-winter afternoon he discovered the jaw of a rhinoceros. He would have continued with the gentle excavation but he was booked on a holiday to Tenerife early the next morning and so he phoned his friend Martin and Martin took over the work of protecting the bones overnight with a tarpaulin and in the morning he covered them with that stuff called scrim and then with a layer of plaster and then he dug out the lump of river bank that held them and managed to get it on to a hand trolley and into the boot of his car. I saw the wrapped-up lump in his back garden, but since then it has been moved to the Norwich Museum. Apparently the rhinoceros was eating hawthorn shortly before it died and bits of broken twig got stuck between its molars, which will be useful for identifying a more precise date of its death.

Jonathan is in his thirties, the same sort of age as my children. He first became interested in fossils when he was eleven. He was living quite close to Covehithe and he would walk along the beach looking for things and even then he must have realised he had a sort of dowsing rod in the mind, a special knack for examining the sand and the cliff edge in a sort of trance of concentration that allowed him to see what other people would not notice. I had made an appointment to meet him and his mother in the West Runton car park at eleven o'clock on a Sunday morning. The day was fine and clear: scudding clouds, the milky blue of the sky, and a slight sense of the approach of winter.

The two of them were walking down the concrete ramp that leads to the sea and they knew I was me because I had said I would be wearing a blue beret. Jonathan's mother said she had to give the address at a funeral and I said I would bring him home when we had finished looking.

I liked him immediately; the quiet of him made me feel quiet. We started walking the short distance to the freshwater beds and I told him I had picked up a bit of a mammoth only yesterday, at Happisburgh where the footsteps were found in the mud. I asked if he knew how those footsteps had survived for some nine hundred thousand years and he didn't and neither did I and so we were none the wiser. I said I had always found fossil hunting to be like a meditation; you don't imagine what it is that you might find, but you allow your mind to go blank, an instrument for looking and nothing else. He said it was true; he always felt very relaxed looking for fossils.

He was carrying a white plastic bag and in the bag he had a delicate little trowel, something a plasterer might use. He explained that the sediment continued under the beach and out to sea, where the far bank of the river had been destroyed by the tides, and there were the remains of ancient forests out to sea, but they only emerged when the tides were pulled far enough back.

I crouched beside him and watched him begin his work. He looked at the cliff like a sculptor might look at a lump of rock he was about to transform into something else. He stroked the surface and paused. He used his trowel very lightly, just enough to approach a smudge of darkness that might be a pebble or a fragment of burnt wood. He talked a bit as he worked, telling me that the bank was divided into four layers and the upper layer was around 450,000 years old, while the base, which was a yellow colour and more gravelly, was around two million.

'I hope we'll find some bones,' he said and not long after he lifted a tiny curve of shiny blackness from out of the clay and this was the front incisor of a shrew. He placed it in the palm of my hand, no bigger

31

than a nail clipping, and told me I could keep it. I wrapped it in a paper handkerchief and put it in a pencil case and thanked him.

We stopped at the place where he had found the broken sections from the antler of an extinct variety of giant deer. They were at the back of a wet cold fissure at the base of the bank of sediment where they had been lying out of sight for the last two million years; he had put his hand into the fissure and had touched the edge of horn turned to stone. At this level the sediment was rich in iron deposits and so when he brought the antler out, piece by piece, it was stained a dark ochre red.

A bit further on we came to the patch of sand out of which the West Runton mammoth had emerged, more or less complete in its bulky entirety; the area containing the hip bone and part of one hind leg are still covered in an ugly dollop of cement. And here, just a few steps further on, was where Jonathan had found the rhinoceros jaw. He planned to come back, to look for more of it after the winter storms had begun to do their work.

He was often silent and soft-spoken in between the silences. He found several bits of bone within the river clay and I worked next to him and found nothing, not even another shrew tooth. He said that people who didn't understand the process sometimes came with pickaxes and hacked off whole chunks of cliff, but that way they never found anything and were causing a lot of damage with their casual impatience.

It took us over two hours to cover maybe a hundred yards and then it was time to go back. As he stood up to leave Jonathan suddenly said, 'I am interested in happiness and what makes people happy or unhappy,' and then he said he thought it didn't matter what you did with your life, just so long as it made you happy. He said he found a single god difficult to imagine, but he liked the idea of God being present in all sorts of aspects of the natural world.

When we reached his house two Clumber spaniels in the kitchen gave us a rather vague welcome. We went into the sun room, in which there was a sofa and an armchair, a table covered in old newspapers and a view of the back garden. Jonathan brought me a mug of tea and then bustled off to fetch one of the many drawers containing his fossil collection.

A chorus of voices. One drawer held the jaw of a wolf, the teeth a milky blue colour and still energetic in their snap and snarl. Then the jaw of a giant beaver, from when they were building their dams across the sweep of the vanished river, the blackened front incisor as long as the span of my hand. Another drawer held the upper section of a rhinoceros skull, brightly white and worn smooth of all detail so it was like a mask a man might choose to wear in a dance, turning himself into some other creature, the flickering light from a fire increasing the transformation.

There was a similar sense of metamorphosis in the ankle bone of a horse that looked for all the world like the torso of a man: the belly stretched and taut, the shoulders strong, the top of the thighs just visible. I could suddenly understand how such an object made the overlapping connection between being human and being animal, between being dead and being alive. It was a perfect sculpture, small enough to hold and yet enormous in the authority of its presence, if you placed it somewhere where you could stare at it and allow it to occupy your mind.

When the Clumber spaniels announced the return of Jonathan's mother from her work at the church, I thought it was time to go and after thanking both of them I took my leave and said I would come back on another day.

7

I met Tim Holt-Wilson at a conference about Doggerland that was being held at the arts centre in my local town. The conference was organised as an attempt to bridge the gap between science and the arts. The main speaker was Professor Vince Gaffney, who, along with a team from Birmingham University, has been working for several years on mapping what is left of the drowned country of Doggerland: its hills and valleys, lakes and rivers, making use of the complex depth-analysis graphs that are produced by the oil industry as part of their search for more underwater oil fields ripe for exploitation.

Gaffney explained that the first suggestion of the existence of a submerged landscape had begun to take shape in the early twentieth century when the new design of deep-sea trawling nets caught not only the bones of mammoth and other extinct beasts, but also the bones of more familiar animals from the Holocene, which started a mere 11,500 years ago. Then in 1931 a fishing vessel working above the area known as Dogger Bank scooped up a dark lump of terrestrial vegetable matter known as *moorlog,* and lodged inside it was a harpoon carved from the antler of a deer. The harpoon was not worn or damaged in any way and had clearly been lost or intentionally deposited in this particular place, at a time when Dogger Bank must have been a fair-sized island or even part of a much larger mainland.

Using a series of computer-generated maps alongside other images, Gaffney described Doggerland when it first emerged from under the weight and cold of the last Ice Age and then took shape and flourished as one of the most densely populated areas in a much larger Europe.

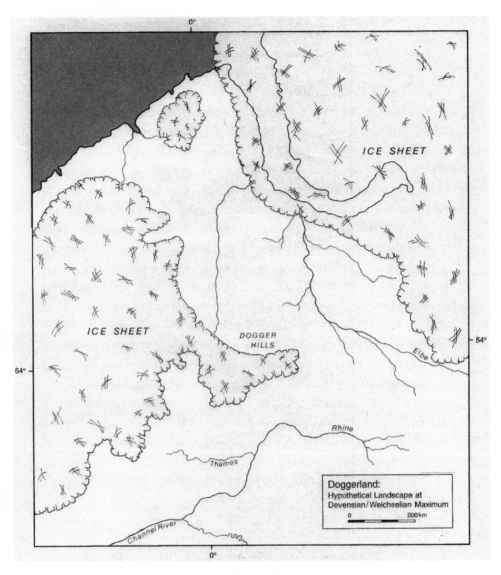

ICE SHEET

ICE SHEET

DOGGER
HILLS

Elbe

Rhine

Thames

Doggerland:
Hypothetical Landscape at
Devensian/Weichselian Maximum
0   200 km

Channel River

0°

54°

54°

0°

c. 18,000 BP

He then followed its slow inundation as sea levels began to rise and its final disappearance when the entire area vanished and Britain was separated from the land to which it had been joined.

The conference also included a display of paintings by my friend Jayne Ivimey: gentle images that seemed to look through the surface covering of water towards the rippled land that lay beneath it, still marked with the footprints of birds and humans. There was a series of photographs of the battered and changing East Anglian coastline as it now is, a recitation of a sequence of poems evoking the people who had perhaps lived in a country that no longer exists, and a film made among the sand dunes and marshlands, imagining these same people fleeing from the encroaching sea. A singer sang a wistful song about what it means to be banished from a place where you once belonged and then Tim, who knows a great deal about the geology and history of East Anglia, somehow managed to straddle the worlds of science and the arts when he spoke of places he had visited along the east coast and all over Eastern Europe, in his search to find out how Doggerland might have looked.

Throughout the day, the audience was very attentive and the atmosphere was curiously intense. It was as if everyone felt personally involved in the loss of a country which is so near, even though it cannot be seen or entered, alongside the loss of the animals and the human beings who had chosen to live there.

At the end of the conference I spoke briefly to Tim and told him I was maybe going to write a book about Doggerland, although I had no clear sense of what sort of shape such a book might take. He said he would be happy to help, if he could.

So there I was, several months later, visiting Tim. He lives in a low, red-brick Victorian building that is part of an old ancestral estate. It might have been a gamekeeper's cottage, although for that there should be more small windows at funny angles for catching sight of approaching poachers. I lived in a gamekeeper's cottage once, in the middle of a wood not far from the drowned town of Dunwich, and it was those oddly placed windows that I remember most vividly; that and the damp in the walls which could turn a pair of leather shoes blue with mould in just a few days.

The garden around Tim's house had a nice ramshackle air, as if it gets on with its own life but doesn't welcome interference. He heard my car and came out to meet me. He is very tall, so he needs to bow his head to pass through his own front door. He led me into a sitting room filled with books that inhabited bookcases, but had also established themselves in heaps and little towers on the floor and on other pieces of furniture. There were paintings and photographs on the walls and on shelves and lots of mysterious objects scattered haphazardly around; the same sort of things that I tend to collect, but here, because I did not know them, they all seemed to be waiting to have their names called out, so they could step forward and identify themselves. Tim said that the bright white bone on the lower shelf of the bookcase was a rhinoceros vertebra, and next to it was a flint scraper that looked like nothing at all until I picked it up and it positioned itself perfectly in my hand, the cutting edge ready to strip meat from a carcass. A broken Greek head, a lump of twisted wood, a piece of medieval carving, all jostling together in each other's company.

Tim is not so well. He explained briefly that his immune system has collapsed and I didn't want to intrude by asking what the implications of such a collapse might be, but there was something about the quiet of him which made it seem as if he has needed to learn to keep one foot in this world and one in the next. I sat on the sofa and he sat in an armchair and the talk was surprisingly easy, even though the subject matter was sometimes quite complex. He is interested in what he calls *process*, a belief that every animal, every human, trees, earth, stones, even a crystal of sand, or a filament from a spider's web, has its own life in the world, its own process. This process does not begin with birth or end with death, it is a trajectory in which there is no finite end. The skull of a dead man is part of the process of that man's life, even when it is nothing but a scattering of dust. A lump of flint is its own process and so too is the fossil of a shell it contains imprinted into itself.

Tim said something about the coastline which has never occurred to me before. He said that when you are close to the edge of the sea, you are in a liminal space in which everything is shifting, nothing is fixed, there is no stillness, no silence, no place, just the rasping breath of waves on the shingle, the wind, the accumulating sandbanks, the diminishing sandbanks, falling cliffs and the energy of the current which pulls at the land to reveal new areas and cover up old ones. Once you accept such a state of flux, then it can be very calming. I wondered if that was why I choose to walk so often along the coast and why I have been drawn to the undersea landscape of Doggerland. I must have said something about my husband's death, because Tim briefly mentioned a tragedy within his own life that happened many years ago. Someone he loved died unexpectedly and for him the immediacy of this loss remains as vivid as it ever was. But then with hardly any transition, the conversation moved on and we got to talking about the people who lived in Doggerland and how on earth I could get a sense of who they were, how they might have been.

He lent me a book by Asen Balikci called *The Netsilik Eskimo*, partly based on a study done in the 1930s and also on a later work by a man who had lived with them in the 1960s, before they had moved into the modern world of corrugated-iron housing, Christianity, snowmobiles and guns.

It can't have been later than five o'clock when I said goodbye and set off home, but I somehow managed to get completely lost along the narrow roads in an area I should have known well. I drove through the darkness in one direction and then I did a three-point turn and drove through the darkness in another direction and still nothing seemed familiar to me, but I got there in the end.

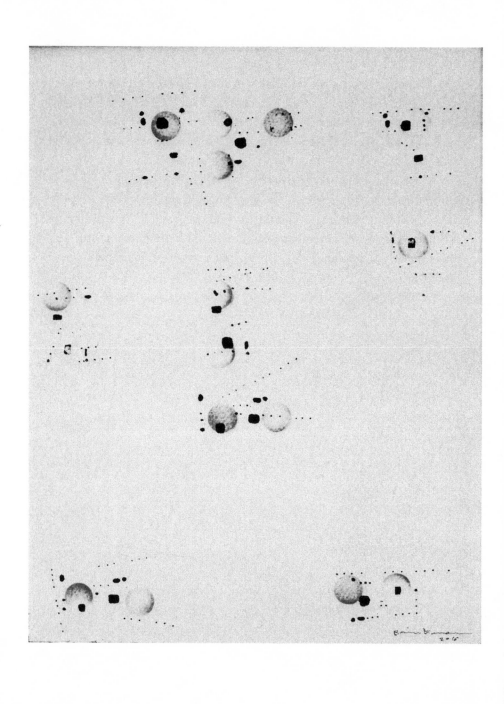

Time Song 3

Everything that lives dies
and everything that lives
has three isotopes of carbon.
I do not pretend to understand
what an isotope is,
but I accept that
with death,
one of the three decays
while the other two remain stable
and from the fact of this simple change,
a date
can be measured.

It means
if I find a flint
worked into the shape of a perfect axe
I can only guess its age,
but if close by
I find a tiny bone,
something from a plant,
or, best of all,
a speck of charcoal,
then I can fix the flint,

to within one hundred years
of its making,
fifty at a pinch.

At the moment
the isotopes take me back
forty thousand years
but maybe that will become more,
later.

The movement of the years
from one to the next,
along with changes of the weather
during those years,
is measurable
in the rings of growth
in the trunks of long-since-dead trees.
These trees
can be connected
in a sequence
of eleven thousand years.
I imagine them in a long line,
dancing.

The pollen from flowers
survives for millennia

after the plant has died.
Each tiny speck holds its own identity:
two wing sacks denote a pine,
granulation and three slits around the edge
denote an oak.
A core of sediment taken from the land
holds the story of what has grown here,
everything declaring its name
under the eye of a binocular microscope.
From that you can also assess
the weather's fluctuations
as one plant family is wiped out
and another arrives
and flourishes.

Beetles have not altered their form
for more than a million years;
they die easily
and without complaint
if there is a rise
or fall
of temperature.
Thus, a fragment from the glittering carapace
of a little beetle
tells you about the nature of the world
it was once inhabiting.

Based on *After the Ice: A Global Human History* by Steven Mithen, Weidenfeld and Nicolson, 2003, pp. 14–15. A single filament from the feather of a bird will tell you what countries that bird has visited and tests are currently being carried out on three centimetres of hair from the body of Tollund Man, who lay within a peat bog in Denmark for more than two thousand years. From that piece of hair it should be possible to know of any journeys he made during the last years of his life.

In my early twenties I made a pen and ink drawing on a postcard, showing a sun and a sickle moon above a low range of hills. Beneath the hills but following the line of their movement, I wrote, *Can a man dream of a country he has never seen?* I had no idea what I meant by the words, except that they seemed to say something I found important and mysterious in equal measure.

I met my husband who died when I was eighteen. He was Dutch and we had four rackety years together with a lot of crossing over from one side of the North Sea to the other. Eventually we went our separate ways, but after an absence of twenty-seven years we started all over again and got married. By then he was teaching at an art school in Amsterdam and I was with my children in Suffolk and so for the first year of our new life we returned to the familiar zigzagging back and forth across the sea that divided us.

We would try to be together every two weeks and during the absences we mostly communicated by that now antiquated system called a fax machine. After his death I went through all our faxes. The thin sheets of paper were growing fragile and taking on a yellow stain from the sunlight they had been exposed to and so I photocopied some of the drawings and wrote some of the fading words into a notebook. In one of the faxes he had written, *Do you realise that from now on, even if we are apart, we will be together?* When I first read it, it was a declaration of love; now it has become part of my precarious understanding of the nature of time.

I was walking along the beach. Sunshine and a cold wind. Nobody and then a couple sitting very still side by side on the upturned concrete bunker close to the water's edge. Two dogs milling softly around them and I was sure I had seen exactly this scene before, but I couldn't remember when.

I had a slight sense of hurry because the tide was coming in and it was possible to get cut off, with the steep cliffs at my back and the waves biting at my toes. Stepping quickly over sand and pebble and the shiny expanses of exposed clay, I sometimes looked out towards the mirage of distance, but mostly I looked down, hoovering the solidity of the surface with my eyes.

I noticed a man walking towards me from out of the distance. He was also looking down and stopping every so often to pick something up. He was carrying two bright green plastic shopping bags that appeared to be rather heavy. As we passed each other I said, 'Treasure?'

'No,' he replied, as if this was not an odd question, 'lead,' and he opened one of the bags to reveal a tangle of lead piping. 'I get fifty quid a week, some weeks,' he said.

'Ever find fossils, bones?' I asked.

''Undreds of 'em. Got me garage full. Three years back, under the forest bit of the cliff, it was all bones, scattered on the sand. I got a vertebra as big as a table,' and he put down both his bags to define the size of the vertebra. 'Sold it on eBay for two hundred quid. Gave a lot of stuff away a few weeks back, to a young girl who's interested in fossils and now she's studying 'em at college and I reckon she'll become a palaeowhatsit.'

I told him I was writing a book about Doggerland and all the lands that came before it and he turned his head vaguely towards the soupy grey of the North Sea as if he was looking at the country I had just referred to.

I felt bold and said I'd love to see his collection and he said, 'Come any time, you can 'ave what you want, it's no use to me.' I wrote his phone number into my mobile. His name was Ray. He lives in Pakefield, not far from the Pontins Holiday Park.

I phoned him a couple of days later and his wife answered. 'Ray! It's that lady you met!' And so I arranged a visit.

They live in a little bungalow in a loop of little bungalows, shoulder to shoulder like biscuits in a tin. The people in the house next door had a life-sized black panther in their garden, sitting upright. I think it must have been made of fibreglass, it was too smooth and shiny to be the painted cement of garden gnomes.

There was no bell on the front door, so I followed a concrete path round the side. The two of them were in the kitchen, close to the window, and they looked up and waved as if we were old friends. Ray opened the back door with the front doorbell in his hand. 'It's broke,' he said.

'Making a noise all night,' she said.

He is not very tall and has a nice quiet manner to him, like an old-fashioned idea of a bank clerk. She is round and jolly, like an old-fashioned idea of a schoolteacher. I had brought them a book and a packet of biscuits. 'That looks nice. I like reading,' she said. 'Ray will eat the biscuits. He'll eat anything sweet. Me, I eat crisps. Crisps are my downfall.'

We went into the sun room and Gail brought us mugs of coffee. I sat in a big upholstered armchair with flower patterns on it. A smattering of polite conversation and then Ray pottered off to his garage in the garden and returned with a little pile of plastic ice-cream boxes. He pulled the lids off and lifted out small objects he thought might interest me, each one in its own sealed packet.

'All this lot's from Covehithe, the beach, the cliff and the private land behind the lake, but I've permission to go there from the lady of the house.' We started with medieval seals and then moved on to Anglo-Saxon buckles. I paused to admire a broken bit of worked metal, some kind of belt clasp, on which the crude outline of a running dragon had been scratched, or maybe etched is a better word. Unmistakably a dragon, and done with a sort of familiarity as if from life. I said how lovely it was.

'Have it,' said Ray. I was rather taken aback, but I thanked him and put the dragon on the side table next to my mug of coffee.

Now lots of Roman coins. The faces of emperors, one after the other. Hadrian, with the word *Aegyptus* on the reverse side and a naked female form which I thought might have been Cleopatra. And then a really tiny coin that would balance comfortably on the tip of my little finger and it was very shiny as if it had just been polished, and holding the perfect image of a round-faced and rather insecure-looking emperor, but I couldn't find his name.

Ray gave me a broken clay pipe. 'There you are,' he said and I put it next to the dragon.

He kept going out and coming back with more stuff and saying how much he has given away or sold. 'There's a good market for the seals. I gave some seals to the Norwich Museum, but when I went to have a look, they said they'd lost them. Lent them stuff to be identified and now they can't find that either.'

His collecting began when he was given a metal detector forty years ago. The first thing he found with it was a gold coin. He brought out the coin from its plastic bag. He keeps it in a box lined with red imitation velvet. It looked as fresh and beautiful as a wild flower still growing in a field, thin and delicate, and it seemed impossible it could have survived undamaged for so long. On one side there was a rather snaky-looking boat riding some rather snaky waves and a king was standing in the middle of it, almost as tall as the central mast. He had a pronged crown upon his head and a kingly or perhaps a saintly expression on his face. I could distinguish the Latin letters that circled the king and his boat, but I couldn't read them because my Latin was not up to it.

'1362,' said Gail. 'Edward III.' She paused and then she said, 'You hold it in your hand and you think, it's not people like us who ever owned something like this. We took it to the coroner but he gave it back. He didn't want it, so we kept it.'

I wanted to ask about the nature of finding, the compulsion of it, perhaps, or the quiet that comes from looking without knowing what you are looking for, but Ray wasn't interested and all he would say was, 'If conditions aren't right you still got to go, because you don't know, do you? When I find something that's been in the ground all that time, it's a marvellous feeling. But the thrill for me is in the finding.'

Ray's father was one of seventeen children. They all grew up in Covehithe, but Ray moved to Kessingland later, which I think was something to do with his mother dying. It was in Kessingland that he met Gail and became a slaughterman.

He spoke of Covehithe as if he could see its past history from having found so many traces of what had been and perhaps also because his

49

family had lived there for generations and it was still the place where they all belonged, dead or alive.

He explained that Covehithe was very wealthy in medieval times: lots of rich people, traders; there was a port there and he had been shown an aerial photo in which you could make out a sort of square shape in the sand. 'You can see where it was if you know what you're looking for; you follow the little path past the pigs, through the narrow bit and then there's that noticeboard and a bent tree and you look across towards the reeds and there's a sort of dip, almost an outline. Boats came right in at high tide and they'd unload when the tide went out.'

Ray kept going to the garage and returning with more boxes, more talk, more little gifts for me to add to my heap. He did have a Papal seal from 1100, Pius I he thought it was, but he sold that, and some years ago he found a medieval well, after a storm. 'A circle as big as that,' and he held his arms out as if he was embracing the air. 'Lying there on the sand, just the base of it, and it was made of wood and there were black things all the way round the sides and at first I thought it was a bear trap.'

That was the day before Christmas and he contacted his friend Paul Durbridge and together they dug out the well. 'A bell-well it were. Double layer of wood nailed together and made from parts of barrels. The mouth of it was at the top of the cliff, but of course the edge was much further back in those days. The people who made it had dug down fifty feet or so, until they reached the water level and the well ended in a point at the bottom. There were pots in there, some of 'em near perfect, and the wood was as good as new and you must be talking six or seven hundred years. It was a work of art.' Ray wondered why they'd wanted a well there in the first place, because surely it must have been filled with salty water. There was no answer to that.

While he went to get more boxes, Gail told me she wasn't really interested in his treasure hunts, but they keep him happy and anyway she and an old school friend go out quite regularly, to a place called Potters for a girlie weekend. They laugh a lot. So she has her fun too.

Ray appeared with some worked flints. He said the lake at Covehithe which is known as Benacre Broad was once a stream, and an archaeologist told him the stream was a tributary of the Thames. 'Archaeologists are a bit like zookeepers,' he said then, remembering the conversation. 'They think that because they are paid by the taxpayer and have got stuff, it all belongs to them. They take over. They don't like it if a member of the public gets in the way and knows more than they do.'

We were moving back in time; the flints were followed by a cardboard box filled with clam shells, all of them stained in gentle shades of cream and ochre and a sharp yellow like clear honey. Some were filled with a coarse-grained sand, packed in tight. 'After a really big storm, the sand can go right down and there's scouring at the base of the cliff and you get about four foot of these shells. You only see them for a while and then they're gone.' He said these ones were two million years old and they were soft when he first got them, but he dried them out and now they were hard.

'There was a chap came with sacks and a sack barrow and he'd collect the shells and dry 'em out and go through 'em with a magnifying glass and he found some teeth of a mouse that was unknown and he named it after his wife. He was big in fossils he was, he had a bone that came out from the sea and he thought it were a pelvis but it were the top vertebra from a giant deer.

'D'you want 'em?' and the box of shells came to sit beside my chair.

Then he told me that once he was walking at Covehithe and on that day the layer of grey-pink marl that is part of the old river bed was smooth and flat, lovely it was, and he noticed these white markings in the clay and that was an animal, about six foot long and four foot wide, and it was complete, but he couldn't tell what sort it was. The white markings were the lines of its skeleton, like a beautiful drawing, and he watched as it was erased by the incoming tide.

He went out one last time and came back with a cardboard box filled with mammoth bones. 'These any use to you?' he said and I said they were. 'There you are then,' and he set the box down beside the box filled with shells.

There was a final rush of giving and I received a bit of mammoth tusk, dark brown and shiny, and he explained how you could tell what it was by the texture of it; two belemnites; a lovely piece of pale fossilised wood and a sea urchin that had been partly crushed – maybe trodden on by some heavy beast before it was transformed into a lump of golden-coloured flint. He'd had it for years.

'You don't mind if I give her this, do you, dear?'

'No, dear, it's been on the side of the sink long enough.'

They called each other 'dear', very sweetly, with a tenderness floating in the word.

I said my goodbyes and they accompanied me outside, the dragon and the broken clay pipe in my pocket and all of us carrying everything else in cardboard boxes. There was something odd with my car and we saw that the back wheel was flat. I'd only had it for a couple of months and didn't even know where the spare tyre was hidden.

'Don't worry, Ray will do it, won't you, dear?' said Gail. And so she read the instruction manual to him while he crouched on the pavement and did the practicalities of removing the wheel and fitting its replacement. I looked on and felt foolish. 'Me and Ray are a good team,' said Gail.

'She reads books,' he said, struggling to undo a nut. 'All I ever read is *Treasure Hunting Magazine*.'

Before I drove off, Ray promised he'd let me know when he next hears from his friend Fred who has lots of worked flints, beautiful ones. He was sure Fred would like to show them to me; we could meet him together.

When I got home I laid out the shells on a long pale table in my husband's studio and they looked like music.

10

Evidence of some of the oldest human occupation in England was found along a stretch of beach and cliff that lies below that Pontins holiday camp near where Ray and Gail live. The entrance to the camp is opposite a bus stop and when I arrived a young man was doing kick-boxing practice there, while talking to himself in a voice much louder than the passing traffic. Behind the bus stop there was a heavy metal gate leading to a large green mound with metal chimneys sprouting out of it, making it appear like the home of a really big Hobbit. This is a landfill site which has become an important feeding place for herring gulls, although I dread to think what it is they are finding that they want to eat.

I drove past a big *Welcome to Pontins* billboard and next to it there was a poster pinned on a tree that showed a photograph of a singer called Travis, described as *the nearest you'll get to Elvis in 1958*. It was easy to see why, because at first I thought Travis was Elvis, until I realised that of course he wasn't. Since I wasn't booked in for a holiday, I felt I was trespassing and so I kept very carefully to the five miles per hour speed limit. I passed little drifts of people, grey-haired couples mostly, and then a woman who must have had a stroke because like a tragi-comic mask, half of her face was fixed into a look of sadness and dismay, while the other half was quite relaxed. She was carrying a plastic bag which said: MAKE THE WORLD A BETTER PLACE.

I parked close to a sign where *parking is permitted for the unloading of delivery vehicles and visiting cabaret artists only* and set off to explore. Interconnecting concrete paths led me past rows of concrete holiday dwellings with names like Heroes Way which must be to do with winning the last war, and Savannah Land which could have been a reference to Doggerland, although that seemed unlikely. There was a restaurant disguised as an ocean liner, and then a fenced-off compound called *Sailing Through the Ages* where a collection of brightly painted vessels also made out of concrete were gathered convivially together. The upturned end of the *Titanic* was poised next to the blancmange shape of the iceberg that caused so much trouble. A yellow submarine the size of a motorbike sat beside a Spanish galleon, but neither of them paid any attention to the *Titanic* and the crisis it was in. The adjacent compound held a fish pond filled with slow and friendly koi carp mouthing the water's surface and a warning not to throw coins into the water, because they would poison the fish.

By now I had reached open and well-cut grassland where there were no paths. The land was unnaturally flat, as if it had been pushed about and bulldozed into shape. I passed a coloured playground to be used by *supervised children only* and several notices telling me to *Beware of the Ditch*. When I reached the ditch it was not much more than a dip in the grass, but it had its own *The Ditch* sign, planted at intervals all along its length; I suppose there was always the danger that someone might fall into it and sue for damages. A *Beware of the Cliff* sign showed me where the land ended and the coast began and here there were lots of extra warnings about tripping on rabbit holes and molehills. The grey-haired holidaymakers moved about in a daze of slowness or sat on benches in the pale sunshine.

I reached a path at the land's edge where a *To the sea* sign was written on a post. The path was made of sharp white stones which must have been imported from somewhere else. A man was coming up it carrying a paper bag, which probably held his lunch. 'Going down is easy,' he said and he stopped to draw breath and to laugh at the joke.

Once on the beach I set off to the right, keeping close to the steep and sandy cliffs. Lots of people had defied their crumbling verticality by climbing up quite high and carving messages into them: *Jesus is Love*, said one, *Sabo loves Nina*, said another.

In 2001 a cache of worked flints, each one not much bigger than my thumb, was found at Pakefield, embedded in this same stretch of cliff, where the ancient river had met the sea. The depth at which the flints lay, the way they had been made and other factors indicated that around eight hundred thousand years ago a band of human beings was here, thus proving that people had come to these shores two hundred thousand years earlier than had previously been thought. There probably weren't many of them and who knows how long they stayed or where they went to next, but the important thing was that they were here, however briefly.

Walking along the beach, my eye was often caught by bits of expanded polystyrene which can look like whitened bone until you get close enough to see what it really is. I did find a small black flint that could have been worked into shape by a human hand and I put it in my pocket. I wondered about my chrysalis from a bit further down the coast and whether it belongs to the same band of time as the little human group and why it never hatched; maybe it was killed off by a cold snap in the early spring.

A man in a cloth sun hat was slowly heading towards me. The light shimmering on the sand turned it into that scene when Omar Sharif approaches Lawrence of Arabia across the undulating desert of the Empty Quarter. He was looking down as if he was searching for something and so as he passed I ask him very politely if he was interested in the pre-history of Pakefield. He was clearly shocked by the question; it was as if I had propositioned him, or offered the first line of a rude joke. 'No,' he said rather gruffly, 'I am here on holiday.'

I stopped at the lighthouse. A notice on the door announced that visitors were always welcome and so I opened the door and called out and there was a merry answering call. I went up a thin spiral staircase smelling of damp and found two grey-haired gentlemen in the lookout, gazing out at the sea. The room was mostly made of glass and it was hot and stuffy. The sea lay before us in a wide sludge-coloured expanse. The men were very welcoming. One of them was holding a pair of binoculars and he explained that he was trying to identify the little outline of a trawler on the horizon. He could just make out the letters BL which he thought might stand for Boulogne, but he wasn't sure. He gave me the binoculars, but I couldn't even read the two letters.

The men said they were both pensioners and they do a few four-hour shifts in the lighthouse every week. Today they had seen a kestrel being mobbed by gulls; yesterday they saw a seal. There was a notice on the wall about correct dealings with porpoise and dolphin, but they had never seen either. One of them remembered how in the 1960s there were lots of seals along this stretch of the coast, the other remembered when the spit of sand that now stretches out for a quarter of a mile into the sea didn't exist.

I asked them about Doggerland and they brightened up with the mention of the name. 'Oh yes, we've heard about Doggerland! It was here, wasn't it?' And together we all looked with hopeful eyes towards the distant horizon, pulling the land up out of the water that covered it. One of the two men said they need more volunteers for the lighthouse: 'You get a pound a day towards your tea and coffee but you have to pay for your own uniform.' I wondered if he thought I might be a suitable candidate.

I thanked them and said goodbye and threaded my way back down the stairs and returned to the holiday park. I stopped off at the reception centre desk. A woman with shiny orange make-up had *Faith and hope and* tattooed on her forearm, but I couldn't read the last word and so I asked her what it was. *'Pixie Dust,'* she said proudly and she twisted her arm round so I could see it for myself. I asked her if she had heard anything about the palaeontologists who had been working along this stretch of the coast and the discovery that humans were living here eight hundred thousand years ago. She said no, she'd heard nothing about anything like that, but a young man who was also standing at the desk and whose arms were also alive with tattoos said he'd been told there were some First World War pillboxes somewhere nearby. The pixie dust woman said, 'Well, I have learnt a lot today, haven't I?'

There were double swing doors next to the reception desk and I pushed through them and found myself in a huge hall, lit with dim red lights that glittered on shining surfaces. On a stage at the far end of the hall a solitary man was sitting behind a long table. The rest of the hall was filled with little round tables, some of which were being used by groups of people busy with drinks and snacks. Suddenly the man behind the long table asked, 'Which president of the United States of America was assassinated in 1963?' His voice echoed through a loudspeaker and everyone was shocked into silence. I realised that this was a quiz.

I wandered off into the room next door, which was more brightly lit and noisy with a cacophony of bells and bleeps and electric sounds and little snatches of music, all coming from row upon row of slot machines. It was a nervous space to be in and I left in a hurry, my fingers touching the sharp edge of the flint in my pocket, as if for good luck.

On my way home I decided to stop at the zoo. I hadn't been there since my children were little. I asked the man at the ticket desk if he knew anything about Doggerland and he said, yes, he had heard of it, but then he lapsed into silence. I said how odd it was to think that many of the animals in the zoo once lived in this part of the world a long time ago and he grinned and agreed. I am not usually so randomly forthcoming with strangers as I was on this particular day and I suppose some of the people I spoke to might have thought that my mind was wandering, which in a way it was.

The zoo gave a rather gloomy impression. There was a big paddock in which three white rhinos, two ostriches and a few giraffes nuzzled about on the shorn grass and looked bored. Another paddock was home to a family of aurochs-like cattle. The bull was very much a bull, serious and dewlapped, with a sort of heavy masculinity and dangerous horns spreadeagled on his head. He was lying down and chewing the cud, flanked on either side by his two standing wives. None of them appeared to be bothered by the flies that clustered in a black mass around their eyes and along the bony bridges of their russet-coloured heads.

I also saw two mangy cheetahs, a family of sleeping lions and something called Lemur Island, with no lemurs visible. 'So I put the towel on the table which is what I normally do,' said a woman to her friend as they walked past Lemur Island. A notice on the door in the ladies' loo informed me that an entire species of animal is made extinct every day and suggested I choose one to adopt, in order to save it.

When I got home I hunted down the address of Bob Mutch, who lives near Pakefield. I had read about him in a newspaper article in which he was quoted as saying that after the storm in 1994 the beach at Pakefield disappeared and the ground level dropped and that was when he saw that an ancient river channel had been exposed, and it was 'packed with animal bones'. It was Bob Mutch who found the first of the worked flints that set back the date of a human presence in England by two hundred thousand years and I wanted to meet him.

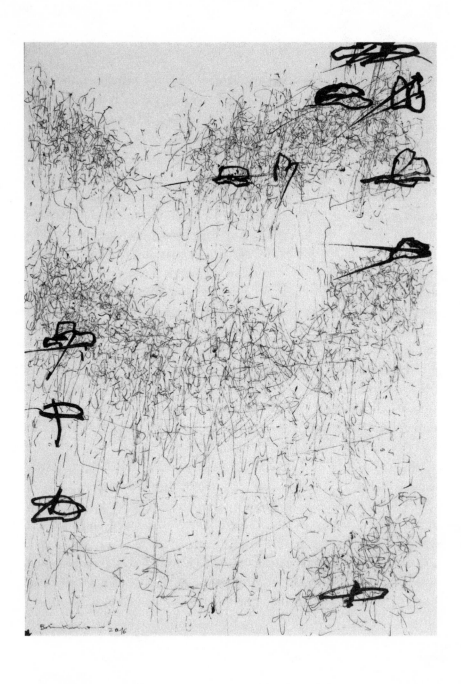

Time Song 4

Footprints need soft sediment
if they are to hold the memory
of who passed by.
They also need minimal erosion
of the surface
and its rapid burial
beneath falling ash,
slow-moving water,
that sort of thing.

Footprints can tell you
if someone was walking or running;
their posture and gait,
their height and age
and more or less what they were doing.

Not long ago,
on the beach at Happisburgh,
pronounced as if it were a haze,
an area of silt was exposed
after severe storms.
Most of the revealed surface
was flat

Or gently undulating,
marked with ripples
like the sea on a calm day,
but one area
below the tide line
showed a scattered mass
of long hollows.

The weather was bad,
rain falling,
waves crashing.

Over the next two weeks
the hollows were photographed
and scanned with lasers,
before they vanished,
leaving no trace.

One hundred and two footprints,
twelve of them complete,
indicating five individuals
of different ages:
a little human group
moving in a southerly direction
across the mudflats
of a large tidal river,
between eight hundred and fifty
and nine hundred and fifty

thousand
years ago,
making a further jump back
in the history of human habitation
in this country,
now called England.

Based on 'Hominin Footprints from Early Pleistocene Deposits at Happisburgh, UK' by Nick Ashton et al., *PLOS ONE*, Feb. 2014, vol. 9: pp. 888, 329.

A perfect three-dimensional reproduction of the footsteps on the mud was recently part of an exhibition about migration and belonging which was held at the British Museum. They were there in the centre of a small room off to the right of the main entrance, well lit and the mud brightly white. You could walk on it if you wanted to, putting your feet on top of the feet of this family group of pioneers who had somehow reached the distant shores where Happisburgh now stands. One wall displayed a film made by the poet Édouard Glissant following the journey his ancestors made when they were taken as slaves to the Caribbean; another wall was decorated with drawings of bombs exploding and children running, sent by a child in Syria to his uncle in England.

11

As a child Bob Mutch had lived on Bloodmoor Road, which was named after a battle and was close to the sea and to the village of Pakefield where the holiday camp now is. When he was about nine he and his school friends would go fishing for rudd and tench in a pond known as Spring Deep. They'd take corned beef sandwiches and a bottle of that bright red fizzy drink called Corona.

There was construction work on the main road and the pond disappeared under a roundabout, but Bob and his friends heard of another pond, at the base of a sandpit which he thought might have been created during the Second World War when they were building a runway for crippled aircraft at the Ellough Airfield, but it might have been older. The pond was mysterious and difficult to get to. It was surrounded by littered heaps of boulder clay and big loose stones disturbed by the excavations and the boys found belemnites and devil's toenails in the clay and soon became more interested in fossils than in fish, taking hammers with them to break open the rocks and see what secrets might be hidden there.

That pond disappeared too when the land was sold to be used as a rubbish dump. It was supposed to be for ordinary industrial waste, but trucks used to come in the middle of the night, carrying all kinds of stuff that needed getting rid of. The growing bulk of discarded rubbish was covered with earth, but sometimes strangely coloured flames would erupt spontaneously from the mound. By now Bob was doing his O-level chemistry and he tried to work out which gases were active: arsenic certainly, but God knows what else. The crops and all other vegetation growing near to the site turned a sickly yellow and nothing flourished.

Bob was interested in philosophy, especially Nietzsche and Taoism, but there was no money for a university degree and so he ended up working as an assistant manager in a bank. It was a steady job and it suited him. But when he was thirty, he became ill with back problems and a numbness in his legs. An osteopath organised physiotherapy and a lot of stretching exercises for the spine, but his condition deteriorated. Finally a neurologist diagnosed spinal muscular atrophy, but by then the muscle fibres and nerves had been irrevocably damaged and he could only manage to walk in a jerky Donald Duck waddle. He was pensioned off from the bank and for the last three decades he has been on morphine: thirty mil four times a day at present, along with the liquid stuff and other pills as well.

The condition has peaks which cause a rapid degeneration of his muscle sensors and then it goes quiet and nothing much happens for a while; but a complete recovery is not a possibility and the bones are slowly disintegrating. These days it's a struggle for him to walk at all and he can't use a stick because there is no muscle resistance in his arms. It is, he says, 'a very restricting condition' but he appears to accept it.

When he was first diagnosed he was still living near Pakefield, married and with a daughter. He was told that walking in sand or wading through water was good for his muscles and so he took to going on little expeditions along the coast. He enjoyed the quiet meeting of the land with the ocean and in winter, once you'd gone a bit of a distance from the path, you'd be surprised to see another human being anywhere about. He began to notice the whiteness of little bones embedded within the darker stretch of the cliff and that was how everything started.

He explored other stretches of the coastline. One summer he was in West Runton, where he met a man who collected things from the Cromer Forest Bed, and after that he went there whenever he could, filling bags with material from the cliff and bringing them home for sieving and identification with a magnifying lens. His collection grew: fish bones, the tiny jawbones of shrew and vole, shark teeth, the best part of the palate of a dog, the leg bone of a stork. He took the more interesting items to the Norwich Museum for identification and gave them anything they wanted to keep in their collection. As a matter of principle he never sold his finds to dealers.

At this point, sitting on a sofa, an old dog sleeping in its bed close to the big television screen, two tame ferrets in the kitchen, a French Lop rabbit pottering about in the front entrance hall, Bob's wife Jean busy upstairs, photos of his daughter getting her Classics degree on the shiny dresser, I rummaged in my bag and produced the three items I had brought with me for identification. First was the little fossil I thought must be a chrysalis, but Bob examined it briefly and said it was nothing special, just part of a fish vertebra, rolled smooth when Covehithe was an estuarial offshore bank. A triangular piece of bone I found a few days earlier is a bit of mammoth's leg that must have been washed into a river and then probably smashed by the sea. The white flint pick, also from Covehithe, is about six thousand years old at a guess, a bit worn, but never mind, it's nice. I liked the straightforwardness of his analysis and the sense that he seemed to be seeing what had happened in a far-distant time as if it was happening now.

He suddenly abandoned palaeontology and moved on to politics with hardly a transition. 'You always need to follow the money, I learnt that in banking. There is always someone behind someone in politics, the puppet master.' And then he said that if he won a couple of million he'd be sorely tempted to buy a Scottish island and live there in isolation with Jean and the animals.

We returned to prehistory. He had become obsessed with the idea that there were more archaic species in Pakefield than in West Runton and then he read *Memoirs of the Geological Survey: The Geology of the Country near Yarmouth and Lowestoft*, published in 1890, and that mentioned the Unio river bed and gave him the clue he needed. He knew that vole teeth can be used for dating a site because they breed and evolve at such a speed, and in a deposit which he thought must be part of the Unio river bed he had found vole teeth with two roots coming off them, which made them much more ancient than the voles at West Runton, where the teeth are permanently growing and have no roots. 'It was a dead giveaway,' he said, 'adding an extra hundred thousand years to the age of the deposit, just like that.'

He knew if he found worked flints in that same river deposit, it would prove the earliest occurrence of human activity in this country and would rewrite history. He started working with his friend Adrian, 'the unsung hero of the story'. Adrian is autistic: very awkward and silent and then he says odd things that make people nervous in his company, but he and Bob got on well, they accepted each other's difficulties and shared a fascination with fossils, although Adrian was more interested in the Jurassic.

This was in the late 1990s, early 2000s. The two of them would go to the river bed area of the beach during the winter months. Bob wasn't strong and he would just prop himself up on the sand and watch and sort out the material as it was brought to him. Adrian always had a bottle of brandy and blackcurrant juice against the cold and he'd wade out into the sea, to sieve the gravel where a river had once flowed. Nothing could stop him, he'd go on working in a howling gale, even if the waves were coming in waist-high. He'd go on like that for hours.

It was near the end of 2001 and Adrian had the sieve filled with a residue of stones and small mammal remains which he was about to throw away when Bob stopped him. 'I ran my hand through the top and I saw this flint that had what is called a bulb of percussion, and a cutting edge like a scraper. I knew at once it had to be a man-made fracture. It was as if I'd been expecting it, but still it was quite a thing to know you're the first person to touch it since Pioneer Man came over from Europe.'

Bob contacted the Keeper of Quaternary Mammals at the Natural History Museum with whom he had been in touch before. He put the flint in a little package and sent it to London by post. He showed me the letter he received in reply: *You appear to have hit the jackpot . . . It is a beautiful flake, certainly human in origin. It is also as fresh as a daisy. Thank you very much for saying we could keep this piece.*

He knew he needed to move forward slowly and carefully. He arranged a meeting in the Jolly Sailors pub on the clifftop above the site, with Adrian and Paul Durbridge who was the flint expert. It was Paul who said that from now on they should do proper documented exploration.

So for a whole day every week, for the next seven weeks, they went back to the same area. At that stage Bob could hardly walk, but the two others would park the car just above the footpath and then they'd help him with his shuffling progress to the sandy shore. Paul prepared a section of cliff leading from where they had found the flint in the sea and he and Adrian dug it and sieved it, while Bob examined what they had found and took home anything that seemed interesting so that he could dry it out on newspaper and begin the work of sorting it under strong magnification.

In the seventh week they found twenty more worked flints and, most importantly, Bob found the core from which they had been originally cut. This was crucial because it proved the flints had been cut here, in this place and nowhere else. But still they knew that in spite of taking photographs of all the stages of excavation and of the artefacts as they were first discovered within the cliff, they might be suspected of fiddling the evidence and so they decided to contact the Natural History Museum again to inform them what was going on. 'As if by magic' a whole team of experts arrived the next weekend: there was one who specialised in mammal bones, one for flints; one for climate analysis along with a sedimentologist and a dating specialist. They put everything in sacks and then they were gone.

The Pakefield flints, along with the accompanying core, were shown to be seven hundred thousand years old, which made them the earliest evidence of human habitation in Great Britain, although that date has since been overridden by the footsteps and finds further along the coast at Happisburgh. An article was published in *Nature* describing the finds and Bob and Paul's role in the work was acknowledged, although no mention was made of Adrian sieving the sea, which Bob found a pity.

And then Bob's health deteriorated, Paul was diagnosed with cancer and Adrian developed shingles which left him with a lot of pain and even blinded him for a while and so none of them had the time or the energy to put their minds to anything much.

Bob paused to think back to what those flints had meant to him. He said when he found the first one he could suddenly see a small group of people he wasn't expecting to find in that period of the palaeontology, but there they were. And then when he found the other flints and the core he said it was 'a snapshot in time . . . I envisaged a family group at a stream bank. They catch a small animal and they make small tools to butcher it up and then they leave. Only a day or two, and they were gone.'

Along this stretch of the coast there was no flint material big enough to make axes, just pebbles that could be turned into little tools like the ones he'd found, and it never ceased to amaze him that these people could survive in such a hostile environment, having to compete with hyenas and lions and facing so many other dangers. He still often saw them in his mind's eye, sitting down by the stream, making those flints. He felt it was a privilege to be a witness to an hour or so in their distant lives.

He had noticed that people like him with physical trouble, or like Adrian with his autism, are drawn to this sort of work. 'It's highly relaxing. You create your own reality and step into it, into another world. It recharges your brain.

'It's funny to think,' he said, as our conversation came towards its end, 'that the waste dump on the other side of the road to the Pontins holiday camp stands on part of the Unio river bed and so all that modern rubbish is lying on top of the remains of early man.'

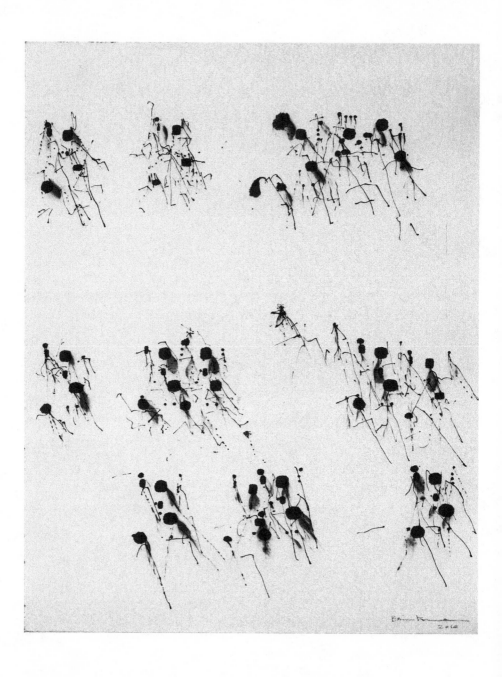

Time Song 5

Two point five million years ago
in Africa
and being human meant
hitting a stone with another stone
to make a sharp edge:
Homo habilis and *rudolfensis.*

One point eight million years:
smaller teeth,
bigger brain,
a more upright stance,
longer legs – better suited for running –
and a hand axe:
Homo erectus.

Still one point eight million,
in a village in Georgia,
under the soil
on top of a hill
alongside scimitar-toothed cats
and other extinct creatures:
five thick-boned skulls,

four lower jaws,
fragments of skeleton
and a few stone tools:
also *Homo erectus.*

One million years:
the Chasm of the Elephant
in northern Spain,
fossils of *Homo antecessor,*
also known as
Pioneer Man.

Nine hundred thousand years
and Britain is a peninsula
on the north-western fringe
of the Eurasian continent.
Two great rivers
cross a floodplain:
the Bytham and the Thames,
and in the mud
beneath much later glacial debris:
human footprints.
Pioneer Man has arrived here.

Seven hundred thousand years
and thirty miles to the south
in the lower reaches of the Bytham River:
a little collection of worked flints,

along with the core from which they were struck:
Pioneer Man again.

Six hundred thousand years,
and evidence in mainland Britain
of brief, low-density occupations,
until the Ice Age four hundred and fifty
thousand years ago,
which left much of Europe desolate.

Four hundred thousand years
and early Neanderthals:
in Spain's Chasm of the Bones:
short, stocky and barrel-chested,
large nose, large eye sockets, low forehead,
the braincase bigger than ours.
A people equipped with clothing and fire,
their bones often broken and badly healed,
they carry stone-tipped spears
for thrusting and throwing
at close quarters.

Sixty thousand years:
after another length of human absence
due to the spread of ice and bitter cold,
the Neanderthals return
across the Mammoth Steppes
of the North European Plain,

across Doggerland and into Britain.
As well as clothes from skins,
they probably have strong footwear,
maybe even snow shoes.
They take shelter where they can find it,
make windbreaks with mammoth bones,
fires from dried grasses and mammoth dung,
use wood for the handles and shafts
of their stone tools.

Forty-three thousand years,
and on the move
out of Africa,
Homo sapiens,
like us but more sturdy,
larger body and brain.
They make complex tools:
weapons tipped with points
fom carved antlers
delicate bladelets, very sharp,
and art, decorative and realistic,
but they can't stay in the north
because of the gathering cold.

Seventeen thousand years
and reindeer move across the land
that emerges from under the ice
during the summer months.

They are followed
by *Homo sapiens.*

Based on *Britain: One Million Years of the Human Story* by Rob Dinnis and Chris Stringer, Natural History Museum, 2014. The recently opened Moesgaard Museum of Prehistory in Denmark is dominated by a great black staircase and as you walk up or down it, you pass three-dimensional models of human beings in the stages of their long history. There's an ape-like creature at the bottom and Stephen Hawking in his wheelchair at the top; they all have skin that looks like real skin and an expression of friendly but abstracted empathy in their eyes that makes them appear like benevolent but still-dangerous zombies.

12

The British Museum Prehistory storeroom is a run-down-looking industrial building on a narrow side street in the East End of London. I rang the bell and was let into a dark entrance hall caught somewhere between the 1930s and the 1970s. Threadbare carpets; metal radiators painted several times over in brown gloss paint; the smell of old dust. I needed to fill out a form stating my name, the name of the person I was seeing and the time of my arrival. My appointment was at two and according to my watch and the clock on the wall it was now exactly that. 'No, no, it's three. That clock is wrong. It hasn't been put back yet,' said the man overseeing my form-filling. I showed him my watch and tried to make a joke, but the joke fell flat. I realised that he had forgotten to put the clock back and he didn't find it funny to think that someone else had climbed on to a chair and done his work for him.

My appointment was with Nick Ashton, Senior Curator of the Palaeolithic Collections. We shook hands formally and then he grinned and throughout our meeting he was both shy and outspoken, young boy and old man in equal measure. He led me up grey and lugubrious staircases and through a warren of corridors and rooms, all of which needed locking and unlocking. There was a lot of silence and no sign of anyone else in the building.

Several rooms contained those metal stacks on wheels that you sometimes find in large libraries. They save space by making a solid wall that can be pulled apart to reveal a narrow passageway. Instead of books, the stacks contained layer upon layer of labelled wooden drawers. Nick opened some of them to show me what they held. Stone and bone, horn and ivory, bits of blackened wood or reed, all worked by human beings. There was something poignant about the objects, if that is the right word. They were like thousands of bird specimens in a natural history collection; by which I mean it was as if these objects had once been alive, flying through the air, gripped in the hand, cutting or thumping into flesh or bone and now they lay as still and quiet as death itself.

Such a huge span of time was contained here, in an anonymous building flanked by designer studios, art galleries, architects' offices, and all the rest of the new wealth of London. This was old wealth, crammed into the darkness. Things that had been offered as gifts to the earth or to the water; things that had been buried to honour the bodies of the dead; things that had enabled people to hunt and to survive.

When I first contacted Nick I'd said I'd like to see some Mesolithic artefacts from the site in Yorkshire called Star Carr, as well as the flints from Pakefield. Now he apologised and said he didn't have much because it was on display, but he collected two drawers of stuff along with a drawer of flints, and carried them like a waiter with a tray into a room where there were several grey-topped tables, a swivel office chair with what looked like a bite taken out of the foam rubber of its seat, bookcases and video surveillance.

We sat down and started talking. His first interest was medieval archaeology, but he began to move back and back in time because he realised the deeper you go, the more interesting it becomes and the real questions about what it means to be human lie in prehistory. The Neanderthals were at the heart of it all, they held the secret.

He spoke of the perfect coincidence of finding the footsteps at Happisburgh. He was there with Martin Bates and the others who were involved in uncovering them as the rain fell and the waves rushed in.

Nine hundred thousand years ago and there was no doubt about the age of this layer of sediment. A few flint tools found close to the footprints helped with the dating and there was evidence of large mammals that died out eight hundred thousand years ago alongside newly evolving species that had just appeared, like the one Nick calls the Comedy Elk because it had such absurdly big antlers. The evidence from beetle fragments and other time dating showed that by this period the winters were very cold, making the area an inhospitable world as far as humans were concerned and yet here they were, a little band of pioneers, way beyond their natural boundaries.

At first it was thought that the footsteps belonged to a group of adult male hunters, who must have moved as far south as the Mediterranean coast with the approach of winter, but then it was shown that the footsteps indicated a residential family group who could never have travelled such long distances. So how did they manage? Did they have hair growing over their bodies, which helped to keep them warm? Maybe they knew how to use fire better than had previously been thought, even though there is nothing to prove the idea. During the winter they must have needed meat, so were they scavengers competing with the hyenas, or hunters competing with the big cats and the wolves? Perhaps most important of all: were they the only ones so far away from anywhere, or were there others who left no trace of their passing?

The conversation had reached a pause. Nick said I could look at the objects if I would like to. He told me not to touch the broken elk bone mattock, which was fragile, but I could handle everything else. He pottered off, the video camera keeping an eye on me.

I began with one of the worked flints from Happisburgh. It was small and black and surprisingly sharp along its cutting edge. I thought of Bob Mutch who saw a little group of human beings sitting down by the edge of a river, napping pebbles into the shape they needed for their purposes and then, once they had done their butchering, moving on and leaving their tools scattered on the mud, alongside the core of stone from which they had taken them, and seven hundred thousand years passed by before another human being picked them up and held them in his hand.

Then to the artefacts from the Mesolithic site of Star Carr. I took out a small plastic bag of the sort that is used by banks when they are weighing loose coins. The bag contained a lozenge-shaped stone about the size of a pumpkin seed. It had a hole drilled into it and so it was a bead that must have hung with other beads on a cord around a neck perhaps. I was nervous to take it out for fear of dropping it, so I simply stared and that was that. I lifted a bone barbed point used for fishing out of its polystyrene bed. I felt the sharpness of its backward-slanting teeth and admired the elegance and fluidity of its line which made it appear like something made by nature, not by man. For a moment I could see the making of it; cutting the barbs, fixing the wooden shaft and then it was hurtling into action and entering the body of a fish that thrashed in the water.

Other things to look at. I made notes. Took photographs. Nick returned and it was time for me to go. He picked up the drawers and I followed him back to the stacks. Before leaving I made a rather awkward request, asking if he could show me the object in the collection that was to him the most interesting, or beautiful. I wasn't quite sure what I meant by this request, but he didn't seem to mind and he thought for a moment and then fetched a Neanderthal hand axe. The flint from which it was made was divided into three bands of colour: a softly curdled yellow, mottled grey, then the yellow again with a perfect black disc no bigger than my fingernail in the top corner, like a moon in full eclipse. The stone was the shape of a simple leaf. It fitted into the palm of my hand and there was an energy to it, as if it was waiting for my fingers to close around it and set it to work. It was four hundred thousand years old.

Nick explained that he was startled by the absolute beauty of it and because of that beauty it tells a story about an individual who chose this particular stone, someone who was proud to put something of himself into a functional object. Both sides had been given what is called an S-twist, which has no apparent purpose apart from the fact that it looks good.

The big technological leap for the Neanderthals came around 250,000 years ago, when they started to make wooden hafts. The stone head for a spear or an axe is relatively easy to produce, but to connect it with a different element is a huge challenge. The work involves bending, moistening, creating the mastic for glues, carving the meeting place at one end in order to reach what Nick called the magical turning point which comes from joining one thing with another.

13

1972 and I was sharing a cottage in North Wales with my old school friend Caroline. The cottage had no electricity and the back wall was built into the hill which meant that when it rained, the water seeped through and ran out across the kitchen floor. One cold spring evening we were huddled close to the fire in the sitting room when a slow wave containing a matchbox, a shopping bag, a dishcloth, onion skins and clumps of dust and rubbish drifted in towards us.

I needed to earn some money and I got a job from the husband of a woman whom I hardly knew. He was a writer who had been commissioned to write a book about how to perform conjuring tricks. He had written nothing but he had already spent the advance. He said if I produced a text on his behalf he would give me the second instalment and he mentioned what sounded like a huge sum so I accepted the deal without hesitation. I was sent a heap of books about conjuring tricks and how to do them and I began to put the thing together without pausing to wonder if this project was a good idea. Over the next three months I completed the first draft of a conjurer's guide to magic with much reference to the term *sleight of hand* which I liked the sound of.

I posted the manuscript to the publisher who was based in New York and when I had heard nothing from them I went down to the red phone box in the nearby village, clutching a heap of coins. I chose to go in the late afternoon because I knew that would be the morning over there.

After a bit of a delay I got through to someone who said my book made no sense, it could not possibly be used, a lot of time had been wasted and there was certainly going to be no payment. I was startled and upset, but in a curious way I didn't mind because I had enjoyed the process of learning things about which I knew nothing.

I was reminded of this story when I woke early in the morning with the dawn not yet arrived and me worrying about these journeys in search of Doggerland, trying to learn prehistory hand to mouth as I go along. I told myself that the answer lies in the pleasure of the doing, the pleasure of diving into one's own uncertainty and finding a way back to the shore and with that I was quietened into a restless sleep.

14

The Mammoth Steppes is the name given to the land in the North Sea Basin that once joined England with the spreading bulk of Europe. It was an icy desert in the winter, but in the summer the area burst into life, the layer of permafrost holding a shallow covering of water which became fertile marshes where grasses and reeds grew and swirls of moss spread out in great lakes of luminous green as bright as neon lights. On slightly higher ground the low shrubs and bushes produced their new foliage and their flowers. Mammoth once congregated here in great numbers before they moved further north. They were replaced by horses and herds of big-hoofed, heavy-coated reindeer that followed the seasons.

This could be a landscape in early autumn sixty thousand years ago, in which case bands of Neanderthals are hunting the reindeer on their annual migration south; it could also be seventeen thousand years ago as Doggerland emerges from under the cloak of ice that has covered it for so long, and now the reindeer hunters belong to the culture known as Magdalenian. To make a final jump in space as well as time: it could also be the Arctic Circle in the 1920s and the people

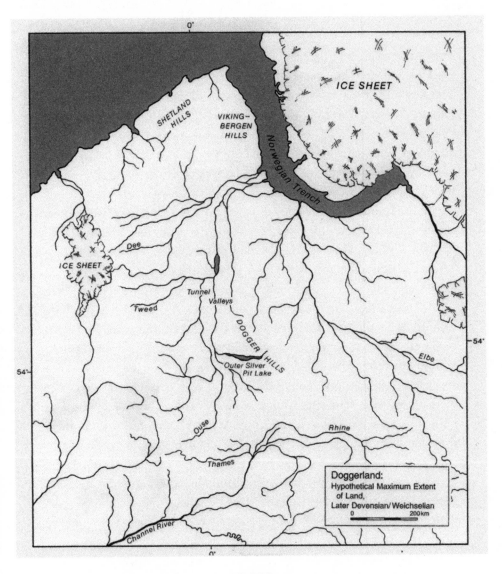

c. 15,000 BP

dressed in skins and carrying stone-tipped spears and arrows are the Netsilik Eskimo, hunting the caribou as described in the book that Tim lent me and in a series of documentary films made by the same author. Just by watching these people as they hunt and eat, make clothes from skins and tools from bone and stone, you get an idea of all those who came before them and how they managed to survive and how they understood their connection with the natural world in which they found themselves.

In the summer the caribou are scattered over vast areas. Two hunters are on the ridge of a hill. They have sighted a small herd moving down through a valley. They run to the end of the valley. They find a place where they can hide and as the animals pass they shoot one or two flint arrows at them.

If the caribou are in an open landscape where there is nowhere to hide, the same two hunters hunch their bodies forward, pull their fur-lined hoods over their heads, hold their bows and sticks upright as if they were antlers and with a drifting, bobbing movement they seem to be grazing, just like all the others. They edge closer and closer to the herd and sometimes an individual caribou approaches out of curiosity or a sense of companionship. When the hunters are in range, they stand up straight and there is just enough time to shoot one or two arrows.

Autumn and the vast herds are beginning their annual migration south. There are hundreds of thousands of them, mostly females and their young: the bulls will follow later. The animals are fat from the summer pastures; their hair is short and thick. A group of hunters gets ready. They build a line of stone cairns on top of a ridge leading to a lake where the caribou will pass. When the caribou see the cairns they are frightened because they look like a line of standing figures waiting for the moment to attack. Some of the hunters are hiding behind the cairns and they make loud wolf cries, so the animals panic and race towards the lake. Other hunters are lying in wait by the water, hidden behind a barrier of stones they have erected.

The hunters assemble on the lake in their kayaks, close to the crossing place the caribou are bound to use. Women and children are crouching silently along the shore, holding bits of skin. The thundering herd approaches and begins to enter the lake, swimming in the ice-cold water. The men in the kayaks throw their spears. The caribou try to return to the shore but now the women and children are howling and screaming like wolves, waving the bits of skin that look like wolf tails. The caribou return to the lake to escape from the wolves and the men go on throwing their spears. When the hunt is over, each hunter collects the animals he has killed, tying them together by their antlers with a thong, before pulling them ashore. A single hunter can kill up to ten caribou on a day like this. The men use their knives to remove the thick skin from the caribou in one perfect piece. They take great care with the back sinew which can be made into cord for binding and holding and thread for sewing. The women start to work on the skins, spreading them out on the ground to dry, hair side facing down, the edges anchored with little stones. They cut the sinews into narrow strips that are stretched between boulders. The men are butchering the meat. They give the children the eyes to eat. Everyone is very hungry; they gorge themselves on lumps of raw meat as they work. They talk and laugh a lot from the excitement of what has just happened and from the presence of so much food. A chattering of voices and little cries. The bigger bones are smashed in order to reach the rich marrow, and the sticky green contents of the stomach are scooped out and eaten as a delicacy. The women cut the excess of meat into flat strips that they hang to dry on long lines in front of fires made from heather. The remains of the carcasses are hidden under heavy stones where they cannot be reached by scavengers.

While their parents are busy, the children pick arctic berries and check the snares to see if they have caught any gulls. A child can play for hours with a snared gull attached to a thread of sinew.

When they are ready to leave their autumn encampment, the people roll up the raw dried skins. A family of four needs at least thirty caribou for clothing and for sleeping under. The skins of polar bears and musk ox are too heavy to wear, but are good as mattresses. Bear skins attract lice and so a piece is always kept as a louse trap.

If fine soft inner garments are to be made, then at night in the igloo both the men and the women wrap their naked bodies into the flesh side of the raw skins, before covering themselves with their usual sleeping skins. The direct warmth of the body softens the skins, making them easier to clean with a scraper.

Once it has been scraped, the women soften the hide further by chewing it and moistening it with their saliva. They stretch it on frames and put it outside in the cold so it can freeze for a day or two. The subcutaneous tissue is removed with a sharp scraper and if it needs to be thinned still further, the men do the work of more vigorous scraping. Children's garments come from very young caribou. The short-haired skin from the caribou legs is good for boots and mittens. The white hair on the skin from the stomach area is used for the decorative details on women's clothes, as hair decoration and for ritual items used by the shamans.

For outer garments and sleeping bags the method of preparation is less complicated; there is no night warming and the skins are simply scraped, making them snow-proof and easier to dry out when they are wet.

The people also make trousers from fox and wolf; they make containers for wick moss from dried duck skins and containers for holding a man's small working tools from the skin of char. Ringed seal is used for summer coats and trousers and for covering kayaks; bearded seal is used for the waterproof boots that are needed during the wet season of the summer months. These summer boots must have all the hair scraped from them: a woman spreads the cold wet skin over her bare thigh as she removes the hair with a sharp moon-shaped knife. The skin is softened by chewing before it is sewn. Seal skin is also used for tent sheets, sled runners, oil and water containers, packs and snow shovels, dog shoes and dog whips, harness lines and harpoon lines, ropes and fish-drying racks. Needles are made from the wing bones of birds and from the strong bones of polar bears that cannot be split and have to be thinned and sharpened with an adze and various knives.

The tools and weapons the Neanderthals made were less complex but they had fire and they made shelters and must have had some sort of needle to stitch their garments and footwear. I have been reading about how the people who first arrived in Doggerland used to lower reindeer carcasses into fast-flowing rivers, fixing them to boulders with thongs, and in that way the meat was kept fresh and safe from scavengers.*

---

*Based on *The Netsilik Eskimo* by Asen Balikci, 1970; *At the Caribou Crossing Place,* RAI film directed by Quentin Brown, with Asen Balikci, 1967.

15

In 1975 I was living in Amsterdam where I met my first husband. We settled in England and had children and were together for more than twenty years and I was again zigzagging back and forth between two countries. In Holland we would often go to a wooden house perched like a nesting bird among the sand dunes on an island that looked out across the North Sea towards Suffolk. The coastline there was in many ways very similar to the coastline here, giving the sense that they were part of a single land mass and the separation was accidental and would not last for long.

When the marriage got into difficulties, I would sometimes sit on the beach and if the moon was full, it cast a broad path across the water as far as the horizon, making it look easy to walk to the other side. During the day when the sea was calm and with the peculiar soupy greyness that comes from the silt of so many rivers flowing into it, the great stretch of water in front of me could appear as solid as the earth's surface, and then I felt all I needed to do was to find the courage to run.

I never picked up anything of interest on the dunes; only white shells that were good for turning into mobiles for babies and the exoskeletons of tiny sea urchins that broke too easily between your fingers. But further along the coast where the Rhine enters the sea at Rotterdam, I might have found old bones as heavy as stone, or even a stone turned into a tool, a horn turned into a weapon. I was told quite recently that there are more remains of mammoth on the bed of the North Sea than anywhere else in the world, apart from Siberia. They are there alongside the other lost creatures from the land or from the ocean; all of them adapting or departing, or dying out as the climate shifted from cold to hot to cold again.

I was telling my Amsterdam friend Sandra about Doggerland and how it had changed and changed again over the millennia. I got to know Sandra in 1975 when we shared a house and used to write rather odd and mostly unpublished articles together: an interview with the reptile keeper at the Amsterdam zoo; a series of conversations with the men and women who stood guard in museums. Sandra said I should meet a fisherman called Klaas Post. She had interviewed him for a documentary film about Urk, which had been an island until the land around it was reclaimed in the twentieth century. She had noticed heaps of big old bones in a yard outside his storeroom, black and very smelly, and when she asked what they were, he said they were mostly mammoth, but the conversation went no further.

Sandra told me about the people of Urk. As islanders, they had been a very remote and very religious community, members of the Dutch Reformed Church which demanded an absolute belief in the authority of the Bible. Fishing was their way of life and in the late nineteenth century they adopted the new boom-trawling method. Long weighted nets were dragged across the sea floor, gathering every living thing that lay there: plaice and sole and other bottom feeders, starfish, crabs and lobsters, all hauled into the air in a muddled heap of desperation. But what also came up in the nets was the bulky presence of the skeletal remains of huge beasts: curling ivory tusks as long as a fishing boat; stone-heavy skulls no one could identify; leg bones as big as a man. The fishermen hated the bones, partly because they caused bruising to the fish, but also because they didn't belong anywhere on the list of

God's Creation. Some said the creatures had been drowned four thousand years ago when Noah's Flood was rising, in which case the fact they did not survive meant they were not wanted in the world because they were the work of the Devil. Others simply found them too strange and too threatening even to contemplate. They broke the bones in pieces if they could and threw them back where they had come from.

Klaas's family were religious, but not as strict in their beliefs as many of their neighbours; his grandfather used to dry his nets on the antlers of a giant deer much bigger than any deer you could imagine and this was proof of his free-thinking nature. When he was sixteen Klaas was on a fishing trip with his father and his uncle and they hauled up a mammoth tusk in the nets. He found it beautiful and wanted to keep it but his uncle threw the tusk overboard.

Five years after finishing high school, Klaas left Urk and went into the fish processing and import/export business. He returned in his thirties to settle there and to work as a fisherman. His interest in the old bones was still with him and he told his fellow fishermen that he would pay them fifty guilders for every box of bones they brought to him and that was how his collection began.

Sandra made an appointment for the two of us to meet him. She had hurt her arm falling off her bicycle, so I drove her geriatric Alfa Romeo. 'If you start braking before you need to brake it will be fine,' said Sandra vaguely. We left Amsterdam and joined the steady spread of the motorway system, heading towards the Waddenzee. As always the flatness of the reclaimed land made it seem like no land at all, just a thin surface of solidity rolled out on to a placid lake or the top of a vast table.

The town of Urk was clean and tidy with an air of prosperity and that Dutch sense of there being nothing to hide in the way of sin or dirt or poverty. I thought I saw Creationists in every passer-by, recognising them by the purposefulness of their stride and their slightly haunted gaze.

Klaas was nothing like my idea of a fisherman. He is an elegant man in his early sixties I would guess, although I am becoming increasingly vague about judging anyone's age. We shook hands and he took us through an open-plan office where there were cabinet displays of mammoth teeth, rhino skulls and other bits of ancient anatomy. Then we went on to his main bone depot which was not far away.

The first floor of the building was dominated by the skeleton of a mammoth which was being pieced together from a conglomerate of forty-year-old mammoths, a hip bone from one, a rib from another. Three rhino skulls were displayed on little plinths; two were from forty thousand years ago, but the third was a forest rhino for whom two million years had passed since he had been on his feet. Klaas said you could tell the difference between them by their nasal passages: the forest rhino had a much broader and more primitive set of air vents.

Klaas spoke of his life and his work. I asked him questions in my fluent but grammatically incorrect Dutch and he answered in Dutch, moving to a more formal English if I got stuck and back to Dutch again if he got stuck. Sandra listened and did the odd translation between us and I took notes. Klaas remarked on my chaotic handwriting as it looped and slid across the pages of my notebook. I hoped this was not a comment on my character and laughed as if to show I was nothing like my formation of letters.

He explained that they put everything they get into boxes and then specialists are brought in to work on them. Important pieces go to museums, but the rest can be sold. Footballers, or at least the designers who design the houses in which footballers live, love to have mammoth tusks on their bookcases. They cost about 36,000 euros for a pair. Because they have been soaking in sea water for so long they are not as strong as the Siberian ones and need to be heavily varnished to protect them. He showed me some, gleaming like plastic and turned a bright orange by the stains of age.

Klaas has collected human artefacts as well: carved bone tools, antler harpoons, and a few worked flints. They are mostly sent immediately to the Rijksmuseum in Amsterdam to be assessed, but the mesh size on the trawling nets is eight centimetres so the smaller things like flints and axeheads tend to drop through, back to where they came from.

In 1985, a captain brought him a human jawbone with worn molars, and radiocarbon dating showed it to be 9,500 years old. It was one of the first intimations that Mesolithic people had lived in Doggerland. Klaas is pretty sure he has recently found evidence of two Mesolithic settlements under the sea at a depth of thirty metres, somewhere between England and Holland. He said it's just a few wooden posts standing upright at the apex of a circle and around its edge, but he's sure the wood has been placed in position and is not part of a forest.

A fisherman called Albert came in and asked if we wanted coffee. He returned with cups on a tray and little plastic pots of the thick *koffiemelk* which everyone likes and sugar cubes and cinnamon biscuits in their own individual wrappers. Albert was a big man with a shy manner and a nervous smile and a look of distraction as if his mind was elsewhere, out at sea I suppose.

Klaas began to describe the land beneath the sea; a vast savannah landscape like the prairies of America, with herds of mammoth moving around, hyena always close by. Rhino and other older fauna, but nothing was as numerous as the mammoth.

I was having to concentrate very hard to follow the Dutch, but I understood that he has collected one hundred and fifty thousand kilos of bones in the last fifteen years as well as seventy thousand mammoth teeth. Albert has found around one hundred thousand bones of mammoth and a sabretooth tiger tooth, which was carbon dated to twenty-three thousand years. This caused a big stir in the scientific community because it was thought that the last of these cats died out three hundred to four hundred thousand years ago. Albert stood by and listened for a while and then he smiled and flitted off.

Not long ago Klaas and Albert found a sixty-metre-deep pocket on the seabed of the Westerschelde and from that they have fished out some huge and heavy pieces belonging to creatures which died some nine million year ago. Klaas took us to see them. The smaller ones were lined up on IKEA-style metal shelves, while the most cumbersome lay on the floor. I stared at something which was the head of a not-yet-classified species of dolphin; it stared back at me from a round eye socket, although the rest of the skull and even the teeth looked like nothing more than a slab of weather-beaten rock. The stone shell of a leatherback turtle was almost perfect and easily familiar in spite of its age. On one of the shelves Klaas had a photo of his fisherman father feeding chickens in a chicken shed, the photo propped against the fossilised vertebra of a whale.

He spoke of how the seabed and everything it holds moves with the tide, rising and falling forty centimetres every twelve hours, and how during a heavy storm it can rise and fall as much as two metres, causing all the sediment and rock to be lifted up and deposited elsewhere. He said that on a boat you can feel the depth beneath you, you can even feel the meandering of the rivers that flowed here and the steepness of their banks; the deep holes and trenches where whirlpools form and where fish like to hide alongside the bones that have got caught up in the swirl of it all. Fishermen know how to imagine the bottom of the sea; after all, they have been looking down at it for generations. You can give Albert a fossil from any part of the North Sea and he can tell where it comes from, just by its smell and the sand and mud and vegetation that cling to it. He said fishermen dream of the land that lies under the sea: they walk over it in their dreams.

As we were leaving we passed a big metal container, something you might expect to see holding steel joists or other mysterious units of construction on a building site. It was filled to the brim with little bones, small enough to fit on the palm of my hand. They were all identical to the bone I had seen in Jonathan's collection, the one that was like a human torso. 'Ankle bones of horses,' said Klaas. 'Forty thousand years old. We have so many we don't know what to do with them.'

I asked if I could buy one and he laughed and said I could take as many as I wanted. I took three and when I got home I gave one to my friend Jayne and I put the other two on the polished rosewood base of an old mirror that once belonged to my great-grandmother, which has a rising sun with a rather surreal staring face inlaid into one of its curved drawers. The fetlocks, for that is what they are, stand side by side, next to a couple of pieces of mosaic from Jericho and a Roman lead dice that rolls in your hand as heavy as fate.

KLAAS'S MAP OF THE NORTH SEA AND WHAT IS FOUND WHERE

- *Krijn*: The large, red-hatched area near the Dutch coast is where hundreds of thousands of bones of Late Pleistocene Mammoth Steppes fauna have been found, alongside Early Holocene fauna. This is also a source of lots of Mesolithic artefacts and human remains from *c.* 10,000 to 8,000 BP.

  In or near the red-circled area known as *de Stekels,* or The Spines, the remains seem to be more concentrated and include tools and wooden poles and other objects which might indicate burial grounds or some sort of camp. Closer to the coast, in *Middelgrond* or Middle Ground, older flint artefacts have been found. This is also where *Krijn,* the forehead from a Neanderthal skull was found.
- In *Engelse Banken,* the English Banks, a limited quantity of fossil fauna from the Late Pleistocene and early Pleistocene have been found.
- Elbows Pit is a quite unique, with only Early Holocene fossils, mostly red deer, elk and horse, and some tools made from red-deer antler, but no mammoth.
- To my knowledge, Middle Rough is the most northern location for finding woolly mammoth, rhino and walrus fossils.
- Near the Danish coast we may find a few remains of reindeer elk, and also the occasional artefact made from bone or antler.
- Just below Heligoland is a limited source of mammoth, rhino, walrus, etc.
- *Borkem Rif* has very scarce Holocene mammals and some Mesolithic artefacts.

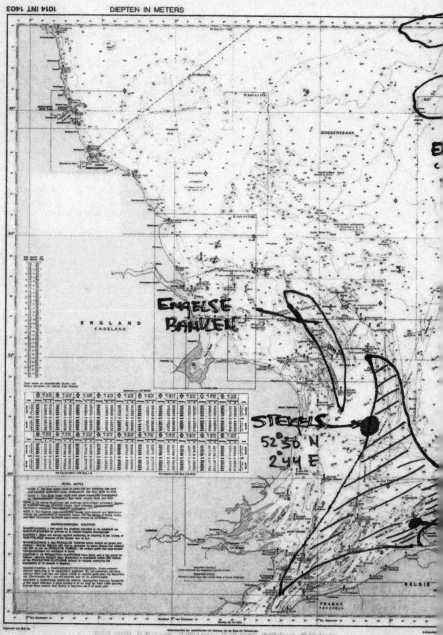

ENGELSE
BANKEN

STEVENS
52°30 N
2°44 E

ENGLAND
ENGELAND

DOGGERSBANK

FRANCE
FRANKRIK

BELGIË

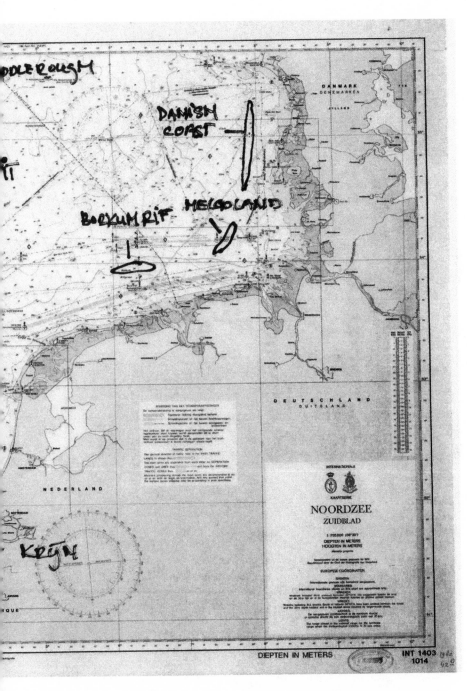

16

Dick Mol is a good friend of Klaas and they have often worked together. He has been a customs official all his life. He lives close to his job, not far from Schiphol Airport. I went to visit him in Sandra's car, driving through the pouring rain and trying to understand the Dutch of the sat nav, balanced precariously on the passenger seat because its suction pad no longer worked. *Daarna,* the voice kept saying, meaning *and then.*

The house was part of several clusters of new buildings all crowding together. I phoned Dick to say I was somewhere close and he came to find me. He is a bulky-bodied man who looks as if he could have trained as a wrestler, but the bulkiness also seemed to imply a stubborn determination, something I suppose you might see in a mammoth, if they were there to be seen.

I am endlessly surprised by the way strangers can welcome a stranger with such warmth. I was ushered inside the house. A pile of mammoth leg bones leant against the wall in a corner of the front hall, where you might expect an umbrella stand. We went into the front room and there was Dick's wife, very womanly and welcoming, and also his colleague Bram Langeveld, who is the Curator of the Rotterdam Natural History Museum. Bram was only twenty-two and could have been their son; he shared the same bulky body, the same look of friendly intransigence.

A low coffee table and soft armchairs and books in the bookcases and bones everywhere. Part of a mammoth jaw with big molars was sitting under a cheese dome on the coffee table. The head of a cave bear was on top of the bookcase, looking very big and dangerous in spite of its helpless condition. But mostly it was mammoth. The area between the front of the house and the kitchen–dining room at the back was a sort of mammoth compound, with skulls and other body parts gathered together. The bones that could stand up by themselves stood in convivial bunches, leaning against bookcases, walls or bits of furniture. The presence of so many bones was lightened, or perhaps confused, by a scattering of stuffed toy animals: a brown teddy bear on top of some leg bones, a little blue and white mammoth on top of a skull.

We sat down to talk over coffee and cake. Dick is a good talker. He dived straight in and spoke perfect English. He grew up in Winterswijk, in the east of the country: an area fifty-three metres above sea level, which is high for Holland, and a place famous for its Triassic quarries in which remains of reptiles two hundred and fifty million years old have been found. There are clay pits from the Holocene close by. As a child he began collecting fossils and taking them to museums to be identified.

When he was thirteen he saw a picture of a mammoth molar and the caption under the picture said, 'The pride of this writer's collection. You will never find fossils such as these in an amateur's collection.' It was this presumption that triggered Dick's determination. He had an aunt living in the port town of IJmuiden and he stayed with her as often as he could and made contact with fishermen, asking them what they knew, examining what they had found.

He grew up and became a customs inspector, but the mammoth stayed with him. He wanted to understand them, where they had lived, what they had eaten, and, if one animal needed to consume two hundred kilos of vegetation every day, along with the two to three hundred litres of water, how did it manage to survive in a snow-covered tundra for eight to ten months of the year?

In 1997 he took part in an important expedition to Siberia. A frozen mammoth had been located and he wanted to focus on what had been the cause of its death. Such a study had never been done before. The creature was removed within the block of ice that held it and taken to a laboratory. They used hairdryers to dry its mass of red hair, they examined everything its body held: the microorganisms on the skin, the contents of the intestines, the casual remains of plants and insects.

He spoke of his subject with a very friendly intimacy and an outpouring of facts and figures. He has collected thirty-five thousand specimens of mammoth and some of them are in this little house with its three storeys, but the rest of what he has not sold or given away is in Urk, in Klaas's storerooms.

He said there is growing evidence that the southern bight of the North Sea and the Netherlands, between IJmuiden and Lowestoft, was dry throughout the Pleistocene, which means it was a solid land mass from 2.6 million years ago until the final flooding of Doggerland seven thousand years ago. At first it was savannah landscape in which the mammoth occupied the same niche as the mastodon elephant and the woolly rhino and lion, and then the climate became colder and the landscape was transformed into tundra steppe. The mammoth was able to adapt better than the mastodon because it grew a shaggy covering of hair and had more advanced molars that enabled it to become a pure grazer.

The water was locked up during the dry glacial period and released when the weather became warmer, but there was always land in certain areas; he said you could see this from the mix of terrestrial and marine finds coming up in the same net. He described what he called the

Lowland North Sea as a paradise for all sorts of creatures: cave lions, sabretooth cats, bears, bison, but mammoth were by far the most numerous. I must imagine great herds of them grazing, drinking from the rivers, and in the summer month of July walrus hunting for clams and molluscs in the soft mud along the coast and beluga whale breeding in the shelter of the estuaries.

Dick picked up the tusk of a baby mammoth and he was explaining how the ivory grows as sedimentation in the pulp cavity and so the tip of the tusk represents the first day of the animal's life, while the socket holds information about the date of its death. From the tusk you can also read its age and whether it is male or female, and even if it was still feeding on its mother's milk. He said that although an elephant uses its tusks to loosen tree roots, a mammoth's tusks were so huge and curled that their only function was to impress the female, to make her choose him as her own, and he became quite lyrical with the thought.

I spoke with Bram for a while. He is the youngest museum director in Holland. He started collecting fossils in the dunes when he was eight and his mother had always insisted that he make meticulous notes on his finds, recording the date and exact location, and that had helped him later. He passed through what he called a dinosaur phase and settled down in the Pleistocene. He met Dick when he was fifteen and his mother took him to a lecture Dick was giving. Since then they have done a lot of work together, even going to the Yukon last year to study woolly mammoth.

Mrs Mol had been with us throughout the conversation, nodding and smiling. She asked if I would like some lunch and returned with four bowls of soup, cheese sandwiches and slices of tomato and cucumber. She set them on the coffee table next to the mammoth molar under its glass dome. I asked her if she has had any training as a palaeontologist and she said no, she knew nothing.

'But she comes with me on my trips,' said Dick. 'We have been to Yukon, Patagonia, Japan. And she is the one who dusts the bones twice a week, so in that way she knows more than most of us.'

I was aware of the strange energy that is generated by people busy with the intensity of what they are doing, being who they are from what they do. Mrs Mol's intensity seemed to come from loving her husband.

Before I left Dick showed me a little bunch of hair from a Siberian mammoth, very red and pubic, nestling in a plastic box. When he closed the box, one hair was sticking out and I asked if I could have it. He put it in a beautiful embossed envelope and handed it over.

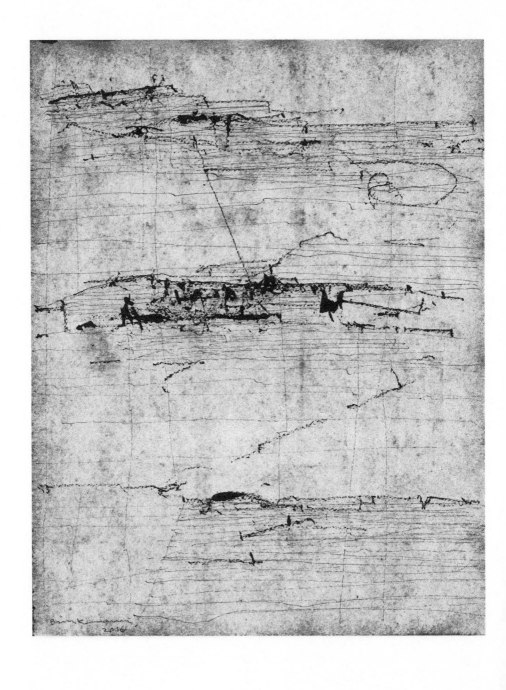

Time Song 6

He was named Yakuta,
after the region in northern Russia
where he — his head, front legs,
part of the stomach and intestine —
was found
trapped in permafrost
on the side of an oxbow lake.

Male,
almost three metres tall at the shoulder,
weight four tons, maybe five,
large spirally twisted tusks
denoting maturity,
worn molars,
arthritic problem in the spine.

The absence of tree pollen
in his dung
suggests a tundra landscape
covering a considerable expanse.

Dwarf willow was his main food.
the thickest twigs, though thin,

counted twenty annual rings,
so the weather was cold
and growth was slow.

The availability of fresh drinking water
indicating perennial wet areas
is shown by traces of
green algae in the dung,
while remnants of marsh marigold,
sedges and rushes
attest to streams or standing water
in the summer,
accumulated snow in winter.
Damp soils such as these
support floodplain meadows.

The fact of the presence of sage,
sneezeweed
and other herbs and mosses
suggests grazing areas
of open grassland.

Clear skies
lead to deep thaws in the summer,
such an arid climate favours
dried grasses
and willow shrubs:
good fodder for large herbivores.

The exact cause of the death
of this particular mammoth
cannot be ascertained with certainty,
but the poor preservation
of the digested vegetation
seems to indicate it took place
between autumn and early spring
and he was foraging for dead leaves,
along with seeds and the fruits of plants,
exposed by the melting snow.

The willow twigs,
though broken,
had not been well chewed
— maybe the worn molars were to blame —
and consider the added stress
of low nutrient levels
in such a land,
especially during the winter.

Lying in a sheltered hollow
the mammoth died,
and a thick layer of mud
slumped over him
and froze him
into its icy heart,
keeping him
— or at least a part of him —

intact
for twenty-two thousand
five hundred years,
until he was found
and carried away,
to be studied.

Based on 'The Ecological Implications of a Yakutian Mammoth's Last
Meal' by Dick Mol et al., *Quaternary Research* 69, 2008, pp. 361–76. I
understand that this is a very similar landscape to the Mammoth Steppes.

17

I returned to Holland a few months later so that Sandra and I could go on a boat trip with Klaas and an invited group of palaeontologists.

Sandra's broken shoulder was almost mended, but then she tripped and broke the bone on the other side in a silly accident probably caused by the awkwardness of compensating for feeling awkward. So I was again driving her Alfa Romeo. It felt even older since the last time.

We were going to be setting off quite early in the morning from a port in Zeeland and Sandra had booked us a bungalow in a holiday village. The sun was shining when we reached this nest of little wooden dwellings; people were sitting on their verandas and getting mildly tipsy on white wine. Sandra had stayed here before when she was working on a documentary film about a murder that took place in the neighbouring village. It was an odd story. All the inhabitants of the village were under suspicion and had to give DNA samples. The DNA proved that a young teenager was the murderer, and everyone, including him, was very surprised by this information.

The next morning we drove to the port and Klaas welcomed us on board the boat. We were the last to arrive; the engines were thudding and the palaeontologists were sitting around eating sandwiches, the air filled with chatter and enthusiasm.

The smell of diesel and the thud of the engine brought me back to a journey I made to the island of St Helena, travelling with my first husband and our two young children, alongside three thousand fresh eggs, a number of live sheep and forty Saints, as the island's inhabitants are called. The journey took sixteen days and when it was rough we lay in our bunks, enveloped by that same noise and smell.

But this was a very different sort of expedition. The boat entered a placid sea with protective islands on each side of us and no sign of a wave anywhere. I had thought we would be going out to the Brown Banks or the Westerschelde from where Klaas had fished up those most ancient stone beasts. I had imagined all of us holding tight while the boat bucked and shuddered and the nets swung in with their loads of heavy bones. I said something to Klaas and he smiled and made a gesture to all the grey heads around me, my own included. I had a brief image of palaeontologists tumbling overboard and sinking down to settle among their own research projects.

The boat was a mussel catcher. It carried curious box-shaped nets made of metal chains, two of them on each side fixed to a beam and at various times these beams were swung out and the nets lowered into the water on hawsers. Once they had been pulled along the seabed for a while they were brought up spluttering into the air. Whatever they had gathered was tipped out into the shallow hold, while the palaeontologists gathered round to look. The first thing that dropped out of the net was a piece from the lower jaw of a whale, quickly followed by the rather beautiful part of the vertebra called the atlas, where the head joins the spine. Klaas said these bones came from the same beast and were ten million years old, give or take. They were placed on the metal hatch in the stern of the ship, next to a coffee urn and a tower of white plastic cups.

The workings of a whale's inner ear were next: a shell-shaped object made of stone that was the *perioticum* and a slightly smaller stone thing that looked like the soft body of a snail which was the *tympanum bulla*. They were too large to fit in the palm of my hand and the skull from which they came would have been about three metres long.

The nets also brought up the fossilised excrement from a very long worm, an early relative of the lugworm. Then there was a shark's tooth and lots of bits of hip or head or back which Klaas was quick to identify. A shiny length of very black bone with a slight bend to it was the rib of a manatee that had swum in this ocean when it was a tropical sea.

I had dreaded being confronted with heaps of dead or dying fish, but not many materialised. There were quite a few spider crabs sidling cautiously out of danger and most of them were thrown back, although some were put in Tupperware containers by a man who was making a crab collection for the Rotterdam Natural History Museum.

In between the swoop and spill of the nets, people talked together. One palaeontologist told me that his speciality was shrews, a species that interested him because shrews have remained almost entirely unchanged for thirty-five million years. I thought of the black shrew incisor that Jonathan had given me, that I now kept in a little box alongside my earrings.

A bone biologist with a mild squint which somehow made her look as if she was about to tell a joke said she had been a university teacher until she became too ill to teach and now she did freelance work with bones. She was clearly very happy with her job. She spoke of the absurdity of separating us humans from other living creatures, especially when you consider how a baby in the womb goes through its own evolution, starting off like a newt with bunches of aquatic gills. She asked what I thought of my country having just voted to leave Europe and I said it made me sad because I had always felt more European than English.

A man with crowded teeth and a very bony head produced a Geiger counter from a box that looked like a businessman's briefcase. He presumed I was a fellow scientist and began to discuss the possible causes of the concentration of uranium in the bones we were finding. He said of course the pH of calcium in bones is the same as the pH of uranium and so a natural transference could occur. The Geiger counter squealed in response to each new find. The manatee made it especially noisy.

Sandra said how odd it was for all these bones to be disturbed after they had been left in peace for millions of years and even the most unexceptional bit of tooth or bone is going to be filed away in a labelled box in a dark storeroom in a museum. She said she kept thinking of the *Antiques Roadshow*, which is also very popular in Holland; people gathered around each new item hauled up from the seabed, eager to know its provenance and age and its value, even though bones are rarely worth much.

Klaas was not entirely happy with the expedition. He said the mussel nets were a new design and they didn't go deep enough or scoop hard enough. Also he would have liked the skipper to have taken us a bit further out, rather than staying within this narrow passage between the islands. He'd wanted to be able to show us land mammals; they were what interested him most and there was always something so magical about bringing them up out of the sea. But he was courteous in spite of his disappointment and said I was welcome to come back the next year.

18

Another day and Sandra and I and her partner and her son were driving to the Rotterdam Europoort. Exit 87000 was our destination.

The Europoort is a city in its own right, but a city almost without people. The buildings are as abstract as big art installations and yet they have their practical purpose. We passed huge brightly coloured hangars without windows or visible doors, only their logos to identify them. Electricity pylons strode across the landscape, seeming to know where they were going and why. We followed long streets flanked by huge tanks containing crude oil or gas, silver-coated pipes twisting around each other like internal organs, while tall chimneys rose up to the heavens. Some of these chimneys emitted flames that were almost without colour, others produced steady streams of white smoke, intersecting the blue of the sky. Both the flames and the smoke looked curiously pure, but I was aware of a raw trace of their chemistry sitting in the back of my throat and the front of my head, like a feeling of unease or perhaps of fear.

The buildings, tanks and pipes were surrounded by high metal fences and well-cut grass. I saw a rabbit eating the grass. I saw a buzzard sitting on a post, observing the rabbit. My Dutch friends said how nice it was to be going to the seaside and they were much less disconcerted by their surroundings than me.

The place we were heading for is a visitors' centre called Futureland and once we had identified the turning we were led to a big car park, surrounded by a curious display of rusting machinery: wheels and grabbers, sifters and lifters, spreaders and shakers and spouters, all of them as big as a car or even a lorry and looking like the fossilised remains of ancient life forms.

In order to facilitate the navigation route of the increasingly large ships that need to enter Rotterdam harbour, a channel called the Eurogully is currently being deepened from thirteen metres to thirty. A notice next to the abandoned machinery explained that two hundred and forty sacks of sand are scooped up every day and then blasted on to the new beach called Maasvlakte, which was our destination.

We entered the Futureland information centre. There were lots of other people here, all of them waiting to be taken to the beach to look for fossils. We had a leader who called us to gather around him and then said we must have a quick look at the Futureland museum before we set out. The museum consisted of a few glass display cabinets holding a few fossils placed on fine sand in the company of shells and bits of seaweed. There were several artists' impressions of mammoth and other extinct mammals going about their daily business.

We were herded on to a bus, obedience creeping over us like a miasma. The bus carried us a few hundred yards and then we stepped out. We followed our leader across a sandbank and here was the newly created beach: a pristine sweep of sand with the sea lap-lapping at its edges and the odd seagull swooping overhead. Suddenly the smoking chimneys, the pipes and hangars and fences and even the rabbit, seemed as far away as if they had never existed.

We were given another little talk about what we were looking for and then we set off to look. There were many other eager collectors foraging across the sand and I realised that in order to find anything you needed to come here at first light, possibly just after a storm.

The odd thing about this beach and what it holds is that everything is jumbled up. The area that is being dredged was once part of the Rhine, and so as well as carrying fertile sediment, it also carried evidence of the many creatures that had lived and died along its banks. Now the machines that are deepening the Eurogully are sucking up all of this prehistory and spraying it out at random across the new beach. For palaeontologists it has proved to be a very important site because so many of the smaller and perhaps more interesting pieces of bone as well as human artefacts and remains are missed in the trawl from fishing boats.

I found something I thought I recognised as a coprolite, a piece of fossilised poo, probably from a hyena, but when I proudly showed it to our leader, he gave me a rather pitying look and told me it was just a pebble. I suddenly felt like a six-year-old on a school trip and I pottered off in a vague huff and sat on the sand to watch sand fleas and to look towards the coast of England, out of sight but not so very far away.

Part Two

Middle Time

The land is a sea in waiting.

MATTHEW HOLLIS, *Stones*

19

October 2015 and I flew home from a little airport in the north of Holland. The flight was delayed, so I sat on a bench in the departure lounge for several hours, trapped in the curious limbo that comes from having presented your passport to an official, so you cannot leave the non-place you have been allowed to enter.

The flight, when it finally happened, was beautiful. This was an old-fashioned prop plane and once it had made a lot of noisy effort to rise into the air, it flew surprisingly low. By now it was the end of the day and the soft light of the misty sun covered the North Sea with a rippled skin of silver and gold.

I had a window seat. Convivial lines of fishing boats were spread out beneath me. They appeared to be quite still and even the wake that showed where they had come from was without apparent movement.

As we approached the English coast, the shift of the light turned the sea transparent. I could look through it on to drowned mudflats and on to the arterial systems of branching river beds that flowed around submerged islands of yellow-tinged sand. In some areas little waves erupted where a patch of muddy land had broken through into the other element.

The solemn white presences of wind turbines stood in rows, a Greek chorus. I felt that if I was close enough, I would hear the words of their song. Some held their fluted wings motionless, others turned them like the slow hands of a clock.

I kept thinking my husband was sitting next to me. I remembered the many times we had crossed this sea and how whenever I made the journey it was as if I was leaving one version of myself behind and taking on the changed identity that comes from becoming a stranger, born somewhere else, speaking a different language.

Staring down through the sea on to the country that lay beneath it, I could easily turn the fishing boats into grazing animals, the wind turbines into trees, the ripple of waves into grasses swaying in the wind, the rivers again flowing like the rivers they once were, the islands emerging and shaking themselves dry.

In another of those faxes my husband sent me during our year of being often apart, he made a drawing of the island of Britain, with continental Europe on the other side of the North Sea, and he marked the area that separated us with urgent circling lines, ringed around with little dots of longing. I realise now that it looks for all the world like a map of Doggerland.

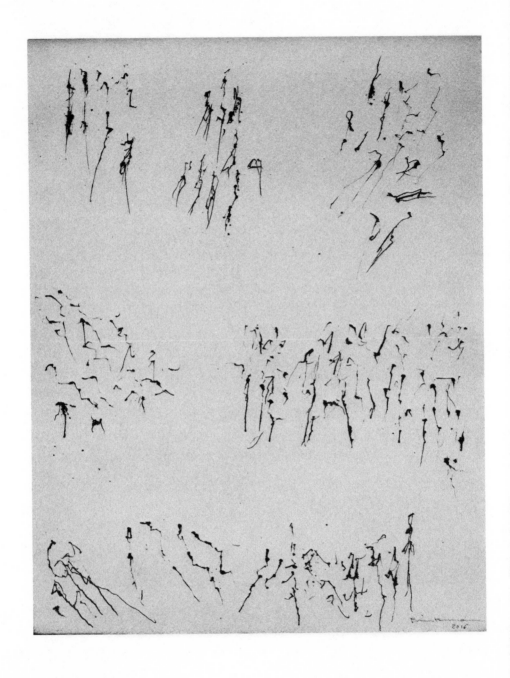

Time Song 7

The most recent incarnation of Doggerland begins
twenty thousand years ago:
the world cold and dry,
thunder and lightning,
a restless wind blowing,
the air thick with dust.
North of where I am here
everything is covered by a blanket of ice,
and where I am here:
a frozen desert.

But the cold is softening,
plants are on the move,
seeds and spores carried by the wind
taking root in shallow soil:
tall grasses with silver plumes,
short grasses spreading in clumps.

The cold softening,
plants on the move,
seeds and spores
carried on feather and fur,
on feet and in faeces,

taking root in deeper soil:
thistle and knapweed,
cranesbill and stork-bill,
wild fennel and wild parsnip,
goosefoot and wormwood,
spread out across the land.

This is the song of seventeen thousand years ago
and the earth is warmer still:
dwarf willow and artemisia
— named after the goddess
who came much later —
a first scattering of birch trees
within more sheltered valleys.
During the summer months
you can see horses,
their coats the colour of winter grass;
great herds of reindeer,
and small human groups,
out hunting.

Thirteen thousand five hundred years ago:
the woodlands spreading
oak and elm on higher ground.
Reindeer and horse have gone north,
in search of open grasslands,
elk and aurochs, red deer and wild boar
move through the camouflage of dappled light.

Thirteen thousand years ago
and a volcano erupts in what is now Germany:
a blanketing of ash and debris,
darkened skies.

Twelve thousand seven hundred years ago
Ice Age cold returns
stripping the land
of all but the simplest vegetation.
Fires consume the dead trees,
grasses once again cover the tundra steppes
and a flowering shrub,
Dryas octopetala,
does very well.
It has eight white petals,
the stems *woody* and *tortuous*
the leaves *glabrous* above,
Tomentose beneath.

Eleven thousand years
and warmth returns
as abruptly as it vanished,
the seas rising fast,
the land changing shape,
offering food and shelter
to birds and animals,
fish and amphibians,
and to humans:

a people poised
between the Old and the New.

Based on 'Doggerland: A Speculative Survey' by B. J. Coles, *Proceedings of the Prehistoric Society* 64, 1998, pp. 45–81.

20

Maybe the oddest thing is knowing what is to come. As the ice melts and retreats and the weather grows warmer, the shape of a country we now call Doggerland begins to be revealed and yet even as the land emerges the sea is preparing to cover it over. I've been looking at a newspaper photograph showing the long crack that is forming and widening within the polar ice sheet and only yesterday there was the publication of a study that says we are on the edge of a sixth extinction, another Big Cut, like the one that marked the end of the age of the dinosaurs. These days it often seems as if the next chapter of the world's story is already irrevocably prepared and we are close to the moment when we must enter it.

But for now Doggerland is waking from its long sleep. In areas that were not covered by the ice sheets, the soil had been held within the grip of the permafrost and as it melts a pale and exhausted ground is revealed, littered with glacial deposits of rock and debris and covered by layers of windblown and gravelly sands. The great weight of ice in the more northern areas has created an undulating uniformity of lowland, with a vast lake at its heart measuring around a hundred kilometres long and thirty wide. This lake is known by fishermen as Outer Silver Pit and is one of the underwater 'deeps' where flatfish and crabs and other bottom feeders congregate in the company of stones and bones and the wrecked remains of ships. Smaller lakes are filling up and spreading out, while new rivers are gathering energy; as they serpent across the land, they plough deep wide channels into it, scooped indentations that can still be traced on the bed of the North Sea.

Doggerland's sodden surface is scored with ridges and white outcrops of chalk that have emerged like the bones of great skeletons. There are also numerous salt-dome hills, just a few metres high and with a strangely visceral appearance. These domes are crowned with little depressions, similar to what you find on the tops of old burial mounds. Some hold flints or other stones that can be used to make tools and weapons. There are also depressions called *pingos,* formed by the breaking up of blisters of ice in the melting permafrost. The pingos that survive today in Norfolk appear as clusters of little round ponds and some of them are still fed by an underground source within the rocks beneath.

Further up the coast and out to sea from where I live, the low-lying land is dominated by the stark silhouette of a flat-topped, steep-sided chalk mass, one hundred and sixty-five metres long, thirty metres wide and thirteen metres high. It has been given the name of the Cross Sands Anomaly and you can see it on maritime maps. The people who came and settled in Doggerland could guide themselves by its commanding presence.

But then, thirteen thousand years ago and just when this new world seems to be settling down, the warming of the climate and all the changes that follow in its wake triggers the Laacher See volcanic eruption in western Germany. I only learnt of this event quite recently when I was at the University of Aarhus in Denmark, talking to Felix Riede, from the department of prehistoric archaeology, who had the white lines of the waves of an unnamed sea printed within a white rectangle on his black T-shirt. He was studying the recolonisation of Northern Europe after the Ice Age and that was when his interest in the volcano began. He has since been working alongside a team on what is called Past Disaster Science, piecing together the evidence of the eruption and assessing its effect on the landscape and on the living creatures within the landscape. They have also been studying what warnings the volcano might offer us as we move towards our own uncertain future.

Charred woodlands and other macro botanical remains show that the eruption occured in the late spring or early summer. It was huge beyond any leap of the imagination and the sound of it as it broke through the earth's surface could be heard from north-west Italy to north-west Russia. In our modern age people have said that a volcano makes the noise of metal crashing against metal, and the journalist James Cameron, who witnessed the detonation of the first atomic bomb, said it sounded as if the doors of Hell were being slammed shut. But in that other time, there was nothing to give form or understanding to the catastrophe that was taking place.

Over 700,000 square kilometres of land were affected by the fallout from the Laacher See and the eruption column reached heights of some forty kilometres, which means that on clear days it was visible throughout the land mass of Europe. The area lying at what is called 'the eruptive centre' was covered by volcanic deposits fifty metres thick, but a much wider area was affected by deposits that destroyed all vegetation and all the life that went with that vegetation. Entire valleys were obliterated, the Rhine was blocked to form a lake and when that lake eventually burst through, the debris was carried as far as the English Channel.

After the initial darkness, the air remained thick and murky for months or even years: ash clouds drifting and settling like dust before rising and drifting again. Ash in the hair, ash filling the mouth with its gritty taste, ash contaminating the water, covering the grasses on which animals graze, affecting trees and bushes, flowers and fruit, insects and birds. Lightning storms in seasons when such storms could not be expected, with lurid sunsets, loud noises and heavy, pendulous curtains of what are called *mammatus* clouds.

Throughout much of Europe the volcano immediately caused seasonal temperatures to drop way below average and there was an increase in rainfall. According to Felix and his team, a similar event is very likely to happen again in Europe and elsewhere within the next three or four decades. When I ask him what he means by 'likely', he smiles a broad and amiable smile and says, 'One hundred per cent; such disasters are the natural consequences of lifting the weight of ice from the land.'

But to return to that other time. Far away from the epicentre of the eruption, birds are falling from the sky, animals are dead or dying or trying to flee in a panic and the bands of hunters who have come to Doggerland to explore the newly rich marshes and waterways must escape, but they do not know where to escape to.

Two hundred and fifty years go by and the effects of the volcano have diminished and life is beginning to resume its old patterns, but then, with a sudden ferocity, a new period of extreme cold sets in and temperatures drop by as much as 6 degrees C within a single decade. This period of cold lasts for a thousand years and is called the Younger Dryas, after the white flowers that do so well in a bare and empty landscape.

21

Eleven thousand five hundred years ago and the Younger Dryas passed with a dramatic temperature rise of 10 degrees C and then there was a steady increase of warmth until the weather was not much different to what we have now and this was the start of the Holocene.

Doggerland comes into its own: lake and pool and estuary; marsh and swamp and river; island and peninsula and the great expanses of mudflats and marshes where the reeds move like water. There would have been the same enormity of the sky that I have grown accustomed to: the shifting mountain ranges of clouds; the sudden enveloping darkness of a thunderstorm; creeping mist and soft rain and the drama of sunset and sunrise.

Woodlands take shape and establish themselves on higher ground, although they are very different to anything we are used to because our woodlands are all managed in one way or another, while these are large stretches of uniformity, only broken by valleys, uplands, marshes and beaver meadows, or by the natural consequences of storms, fire or disease. I've been told of a place called Białowieża on the border of Poland and White Russia that is said to mirror the woodlands of Doggerland most closely, although the person who told me about it had tried but failed to get there.

It is hard to imagine the density of life within this landscape because we have drifted so far away from a world where so many varieties of species can be supported in huge numbers. I have watched starlings thickening the evening sky, seals gathered in their breeding colonies, an exodus of toads too numerous to count; but every year there is less to see and my memory tries its best to forget what it has known, for fear of being made too sad by the reality of the loss. We learn to grow accustomed to the absences, because it seems we have no choice.

In that other time along the intricate northern coastline of Doggerland, the glittering expanses of mud and sand are stippled with worm casts and made electric by jumping sand fleas and crabs, shrimps and all the other small creatures that are food for the bigger creatures.

The air is thick with the sound of birds: curlews' laments, whimbrels' babbling in seven notes; the triple call of redshank and greenshank, the soft twickering of sanderlings, the rattle of turnstones. They go on crying into the dusk, when the night birds join them and eventually take over. The darkness echoes with what it contains.

If this is spring then the migratory birds have arrived: barnacle geese and greylag geese turn the sky black, their pulsating cries so loud and determined you can't hear yourself shout. Whooper swans and Bewick's swans, necks outstretched, their wingbeats and their bugling calls creating two distinct layers of sound. And then all the rest: stork, crane, spoonbill, pelican, a long list whose being here is recorded in the little scatterings of bones that have survived them.

Where the shallow sea begins, the silver eel move in droves as if they are fast currents of water within the water. Terns, their heads at a stark right angle to their bodies, plummet like falling stars to snatch at them. Gull, cormorant and gannet, shag and guillemot and all the others: a dizzy crowd, eating and preening, conversing and competing.

If this is spring, fish are spawning in the sea; you see the ripple of bellies as they turn in the sunlight. Further out and dolphins are leaping in acrobatic arcs, an intimate smile creased on their faces. The white whales known as beluga move in droves, seals loll about in great restless heaps along a sandbank where they can keep their young safe. Some of them are singing; the fat of their bodies ripples under the shining fur.

Animals are always near, some among the woods of the higher ground, others close to the sea and the rivers that run into the sea. The stubby-faced shaggy horses and the reindeer have gone and the big-horned aurochs are diminishing, but bear, deer and wild boar are numerous, alongside fox and wolf, otter and beaver, polecat and weasel, mice and red squirrel, vole and shrew and hedgehog. The hum of mosquitoes. A carcass moves with the maggots inhabiting its flesh.

People are at the water's edge, a small group of them among the other living creatures and, like the others, busy with staying alive. They know how to hunt and forage; how to make fires and weapons, canoes, wooden shelters, traps and weirs. They have ceremonies to bury their dead and ceremonies to offer gifts to the mystery of the world that they inhabit. All this is not so long ago when you think of everything that has gone before, but it is a huge stretch of time when you think of everything that must come after.

22

The book that impressed me so much when I was living on the farm was *Specimens of Bushman Folklore* compiled by Wilhelm Bleek and his sister-in-law Lucy Lloyd. It was first published in Cape Town in 1911.

Bleek was born in Berlin in 1827. He graduated with a doctorate in linguistics and then focused his attention on African languages. In 1855 he went to the Cape to help compile a Zulu grammar and in that same year he heard about a race of people known under the general term of Bushmen, though now they are called the San.

The Boers used to go hunting for the San with the same spirit of bloody adventure with which they went hunting for lions and rhinoceros, and many of those who were not killed were sent to the penal colonies, accused of stealing livestock. Bleek's first contact was with prisoners on

Robben Island and the Cape Town Gaol and House of Correction in 1857. You see them in the photographs, their bodies enclosed in fusty, ill-fitting European garments, their eyes fixed in a haunted and inward gaze.

In 1862 Bleek married Jemima Lloyd, who had come to the Cape with her sister Lucy, and in 1866 he was introduced to two |Xam-speaking San, prisoners in the Cape Town prison, who came from the most remote desert regions. They began to help him to compile a list of words and sentences and an alphabetic vocabulary of their language.

By 1870, working together with his sister-in-law Lucy, he received permission to bring a young man called ||a|kunta from the prison to stay at his home in Mowbray. There was also an older prisoner called ||kabbo who became Bleek and Lloyd's first real teacher, explaining the beliefs and traditions of his people. Over the following years members of ||kabbo's family and other |Xam families came to live at the house in Mowbray, all willing to tell the stories of their people and the culture to which they had belonged until the disaster of colonisation began to wipe out everything that mattered to them.

When Bleek died in 1875 Lucy Lloyd took over the completion of the huge task they had set themselves, making sure that the archive they had collected was preserved.

Bleek and Lloyd worked primarily as linguists when they took on the challenge of recording an ancient language that did not easily or directly translate into German or English. They did not try to turn the |Xam stories into westernised folk tales, but painstakingly produced accurate parallel texts that provide a vivid record of the halting repetitions and hesitations of human speech and the complexity of a system of beliefs, customs and memories.

The |Xam allow one to see the world with different eyes. People are animals and animals are people; a man becomes a lion, a lion becomes a man. A praying mantis is as important as an old woman, as a young child, as an ostrich; they have equal status. The wind is a person and so are the moon and the stars, trees and stones and water. Everything speaks in its own voice and can be understood, even if what it says has the shifting confusion of a dream.

Now, as I try to pull closer to the people of the Mesolithic who lived in Doggerland, I keep turning to the |Xam, in the hope that their words can help me to understand the distant mystery of a way of life that is so different to anything I have known.

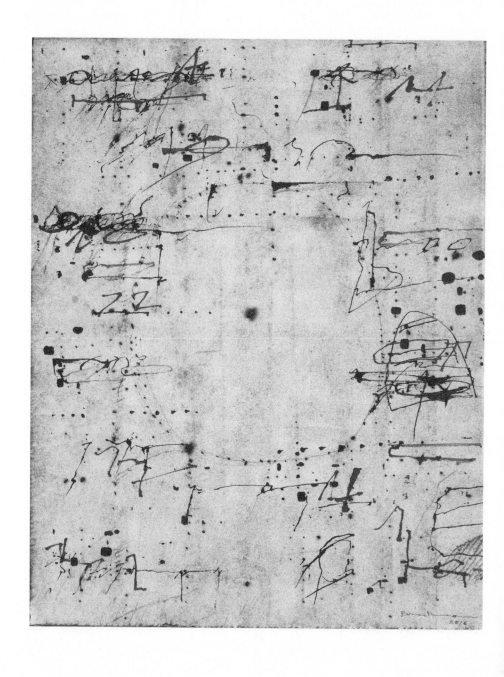

Time Song 8

When a person's heart aches the person says,
'Let a lion take this person, let him vanish from our house!'
and the lion hears
and the darkness falls
and the lion stealthily approaches him
and takes hold of him and kills him and he dies
and vanishes from our house.

This month he was dead;
and this month he was dead;
this, the fourth month Ixue went
and today, this day,
ixue went into the lion's house.
This day,
ixue speaks like the lion
and the lion understands.

told by |inanne and Tamme

Lucy Lloyd notebooks 113:9324–30, quoted in *Claim to the Country: The Archive of Wilhelm Bleek and Lucy Lloyd* by Pippa Skotnes, Jacana Media Ltd and Ohio University Press, 2007.

My anthropologist friend Hugh Brody says that the hunter-gatherers of the Arctic Circle and the Dene Nation of British Columbia with whom he lived for several years, along with the San who came to stay with Bleek and his family, the Neanderthals who followed the reindeer and the hunter-gatherers who lived in Doggerland all share what he calls 'porous boundaries' in their connection between the living and the dead and between animals and humans, the animate and the inanimate.

23

Professor Bryony Coles is the person who gave Doggerland its name. I met her in the central foyer of the British Museum. My bag had been checked for sharp objects in case I wanted to create havoc and I had set my back against a marble pillar: an island within the flowing river of visitors. She was wearing a red wool jacket and strong walking boots. I had imagined her to be taller and more severe, but that was just the muddle of preconception from having seen a head-and-shoulders photograph on her university website.

She is a friendly woman, humorous and alert. We headed for the museum café, the smell of things baking directing us as we walked past early Greece and a bit of Abyssinia. I was tempted to stretch out my hand to run it across the figure of a king with a solid tubular beard, his great chest fused into the block of stone from which he was carved, as if the stone and the flesh were equally immutable.

We ordered tea and a muffin dotted with a stain of blueberries that made me think of a short film I had watched a couple of nights before, which followed a year on a newly established nature reserve in Holland. The place tries to re-create the Mesolithic environment, with aurochs-like cattle and stocky, broad-faced horses, alongside deer, hare and beaver and a profusion of birds. Everything is left to itself to proliferate and to struggle to survive and in winter the flat landscape is littered with cold corpses and whatever is interested in feeding from them. There is an autumn scene in which a noisy flock of starlings is feasting on elderberries and then settling on the backs of the horses, spattering their shaggy dun-coloured coats with purple-black stains. Same colour as the blueberries in the muffins.

In the 1980s Bryony's husband was studying Swedish rock carvings and she often joined him on his research trips, crossing the North Sea on the ferry which doesn't run any more. There was a big map of the depths of the sea on the ship's wall and she was drawn to the island shape of Dogger Bank, so close to the surface compared with everywhere else, so she would wonder what lay on the seabed beneath and what sort of an environment it once had been, before the waters rose to hide it from view.

Her first awareness of the possibility of a much larger submerged land mass came on a seaside holiday in Brittany when she saw mammoth bones for sale in a little shop. Later she met Professor Leendert Louwe Kooijmans from the Leiden museum where they had a collection of all sorts of bones and human artefacts fished up by Dutch trawlers from the Brown Banks. Someone mentioned the discovery of what appeared to be a worked flint and flint core, found during oil exploration north of the Shetlands, and she wondered how on earth that had got there. The implications of all this settled in her mind.

There was good research going on at that time and geographers studying sea-level changes after the last Ice Age were beginning to become aware that it was not just a question of mapping contours; what had to be taken into account was the reaction of entire land masses when the weight of the ice dropped from them as it melted. Some areas would have been flooded, but others would rise up like great waking beasts no longer trapped by the burden that had held them down. 'A bouncy castle,' she said, which rather startled me, but then she added, 'Soft geology,' which sounded like a rather loose and modern scientific term. The combination of images made me able to see the slow shifting of the face of the earth and I had a brief memory of standing on a

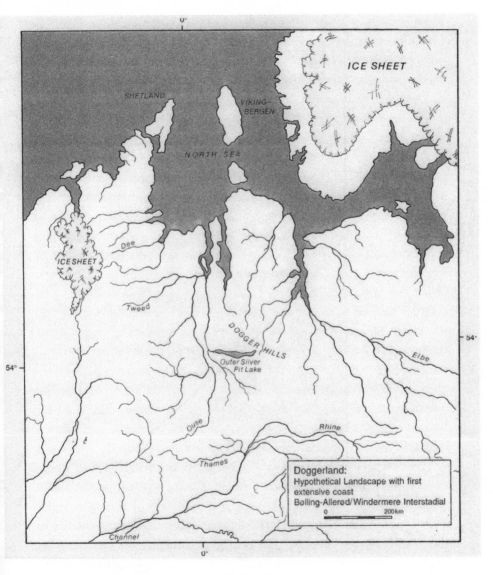

c. 13,500 BP

quaking bog in Wales, ages ago. I was high on magic mushrooms and, with the sense of revelation that can come from such stuff, I suddenly understood that the world itself was a living creature and I could feel its heartbeat and hear its laboured breath.

By now what was left of the tea was cold and the muffins were reduced to a few crumbs. We moved back to Doggerland. For a long while there had been the theory of a land bridge, imagined as a wide causeway connecting Britain to Europe, with people and animals crossing over it – like the chicken – just in order to reach the other side. Bryony was increasingly persuaded that it was a large and inhabited country in its own right. In the early 1990s she was able to follow her hunch when she was awarded a research grant to make a two-year study of British wetland archaeology and its relationship with the submerged landscape of the North Sea.

She needed to find a name for the place she was looking for and she chose Doggerland because that put it alongside England and the Netherlands, Jutland, Friesland, Zeeland and all the other lands within the sea. She liked the etymology of *dogger*, which seems to derive from the Danish word *dag*, meaning dagger. The pliable stems of dogwood were used by Mesolithic peoples for making fish-traps, while the hard heart-wood was used for spears and indeed for a type of dagger. On top of that, dogwood used to grow on Dogger Bank.

She worked on a hypothetical map, using sonar evidence of steep-sided tunnel valleys as indicators for the flow of rivers in a time when those rivers were flowing. The modern distribution of certain varieties of freshwater fish helped to suggest where they might have met with the sea. The true extent of that land mass was given extra credibility from studies of a little primula flower which only grows in Yorkshire and must have migrated from Eastern Europe before Doggerland was lost, while the distribution of field voles with different evolutionary features on either side of Hadrian's Wall indicated a connection with Western Europe. In this way the map began to take shape and the land it described grew bigger and bigger. There was and still is a lot of contention as to whether the couse of the Thames originally went northwards, and only changed direction when the chalk cliffs in the south were broken through eight thousand years ago, connecting the Channel with the North Sea, but that was not Bryony's concern.

She spoke about the density of life that must have been concentrated in the northern coastal regions of Doggerland, an area where there was an all-year food supply very similar to what is found among the coastal hunting and fishing communities in British Columbia. These people were able to form a sedentary society, because the food they needed for their survival came to them, each in its own season, from the arrival of the spawning salmon, the migrating birds, the grazing animals.

I asked her where I should go to get close to an idea of what Doggerland was like. She said that although there are a few places in Britain, so much of the land has been drained and altered beyond recognition and so many of the sites were lost under the rising sea levels, but in Denmark, where the bouncy-castle effect lifted the land up once the weight of the ice had gone, there are still several marshy landscapes that have a lot in common with that other time, like the one near the village of Tollund which has held the almost perfectly preserved bodies of the dead within the mix of peat and acid water, along with the clothes they were wearing when they died and even the simple meal they had eaten before their death some two thousand years ago. And if I wanted to get a sense of the earlier hunter-gatherers who established themselves in the area when the land had emerged from under the ice, then I should go to see the burials from a place called Vedbaek, and there were other important sites lying in the very shallow waters of the North Sea: Tybrind Vig and Kalo Vig in Denmark, and Tagerup in Sweden.

And then to beavers. She apologised that these days, all her attention is on beavers. It started when she was at a conference in London and her husband was at a conference in Canada and they had been trying to work out the nature of mysterious cutting marks that had been found on some ancient pieces of wood. They couldn't have been made by a stone axe, it looked more as if they had been made with a penknife, but at a time before metal had been discovered. She showed photos of the marks to two Russians during the coffee break and without any hesitation they said, *Beaver!* Later her husband contacted her to say the Canadians who looked at the marks had also said, *Beaver!*

She is interested in the interaction between beavers and humans. Beaver bones have been found in the North Sea, alongside all the other creatures rumbling around there. They were present in the Mesolithic site of Star Carr, up in Yorkshire, and on the Somerset Levels. It had been presumed they were only useful for the food and fur they provided, but then Bryony heard something that made her doubt this was the only connection. Following her hunch she went to spend three weeks a year for several years in an area in the south of France, observing a colony of beavers that had established themselves close to a main road. She could only go in the spring or autumn because in the summer there were too many leaves on the trees obscuring her view. Until then it had been thought that European beavers don't make dams, but she was able to prove they do and this would have made them very useful from a human point of view. She wrote a paper suggesting that during the

Mesolithic period and later, beavers provided humans with dead wood for burning, bridges for crossing over streams, and beaver ponds which trapped silt and organic matter, attracting an explosion of plant and animal life, birds, fish and reptiles.

There was a story told by a member of the Dene Nation in north-west Canada and Bryony promised to look it up for me because although it related to another land mass and another time, it explained the closeness between hunter-gatherers and beavers and she could imagine the same story being told in Doggerland. She sent me the text shortly after our meeting and I turned it into a time song.

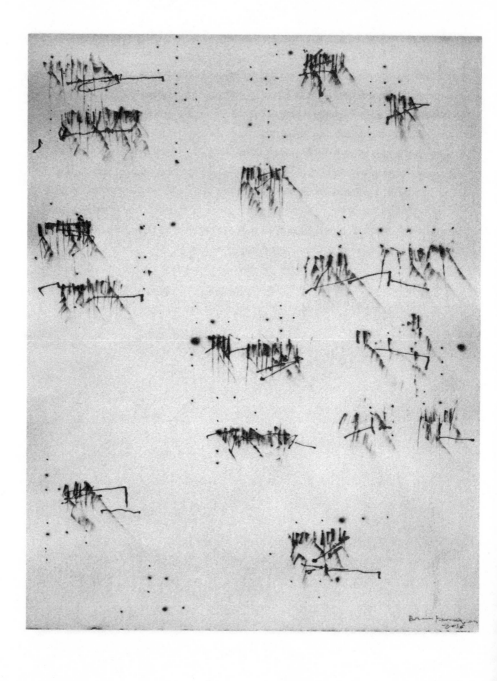

Time Song 9

A young woman,
she has been fasting
for a long time,
her face is painted black.

She wanders far off,
she meets a man
standing upright,
she goes with him
to his home by a lake.

She becomes his wife,
she forgets her parents.
In the spring she gives birth
to four children.

She works
making mats and bags.
She has every kind of food
from her husband,
every kind of fish
and small animal.
She has firewood.

One day a human man
passes by,
and then the woman knows
she has married a beaver.

She has more children,
every spring she has more.
The human people
kill the young beavers,
but they do not really kill them
because the young beavers
come home again.

The beavers in this time
are very numerous,
they are fond of the human people,
they are fond of the gifts the human people give them,
and even if they are killed
they are not really dead.

When they were growing old
the woman's husband said,
'I am going away to some other land,
it is time for you to go back home.
Remain here in my house.
Human people will come.
You must speak to them.'

The woman stayed in the house
making twine.
A human man arrived,
he sat on the roof.
The woman picked up a piece of wood
and made a tapping noise
so he could know she was there.

'Who is this?' he said.
'It is I,' she said,
'I wish to get out.
Long ago I was taken by the beaver.
Please break into this beaver house.'

The man began to break through the roof.
He reached his hand in,
he felt the woman,
he felt her head,
her ears,
her ear-rings.
When the hole was wide enough,
she stepped out.
Her head was white,
she wore beautiful clothes,
her cloak was worked with beads.
She told of what had happened.

The woman went to live with her sister
who took care of her.
She used to say,
'Never speak badly of a beaver.
If you speak badly of a beaver
you will not be able to kill it.'

That is why people
never say bad things about the beaver,
especially when they mean to go hunting.
They know that if they never say bad things,
they will be much loved by the beaver,
they will be held in the mind of the beaver
and they will have luck,
when killing beavers.

Based on 'The Woman Who Married a Beaver' in Thomas W. Overholt and J. Baird Callicott, *Clothed-in-Fur and Other Tales: An Introduction to the Ojibwa World View*, 1982, quoted by Roberta Robin Dods, 'Wondering the Wetland: Archaeology through the Lens of Myth and Metaphor in Northern Boreal Canada', *Journal of Wetland Archaeology* 3, 2003, pp. 17–36.

In a film called *Hunters and Bombers*, made by Hugh Brody about the Innu, there's a scene in which you see a young child sleeping with a young beaver in her arms, both of them looking very comfortable and contented, while outside a woman is cooking beaver meat in a pot over a fire.

24

I dream of animals much more than I dream of people. Early this morning, I entered the remembered image of the shed that stands in this garden and there was a greenfinch as big as a chicken perched disconsolately on a white high chair. The bird's feathers were beautiful, a shimmering rainbow that seemed to contain all the permutations of the spectrum within a single colour. I went to the house to fetch it some food and when I got back it had knocked over a glass of water and I added bread to the water and woke up.

My notebooks are filled with such encounters. I am carrying a mouse with her babies, I am lying in the soft embrace of a tabby cat, birds roost among my clothes; three snakes swim in a wine glass and I meet seals and large fish. Even the dark and vaguely threatening buildings in which I often find myself tend to be occupied by large beasts: a couple of rhinoceros recently, but there have also been lion and bison and even a hippopotamus.

When I woke from the dream of a green bird someone on the radio was talking about human language and how it is probably much older than we ever thought it was: one and a half million years was his estimation, instead of the one hundred thousand which is the more familiar number given by Noam Chomsky and others. The man who was talking was called Daniel Everett, and he had been living with the peoples in the Amazon rainforests for many years. He said language does not require syntax – the grammatical arrangement and sequence of words – all it needs is a sound as a symbol of something we can all see, whether that something is a bird in a dream or a tree in the waking life or the fact of death.

25

Bryony had told me to contact Professor Leendert Louwe Kooijmans, a retired Dutch professor who specialised in the Post Glacial period in Northern Europe. I wrote to him and we arranged to meet in a café in Arnhem. It's a town I know quite well because my ex-husband's parents used to live close by. They were involved in the Resistance during the last war and tried to warn the Allies against the Arnhem landings, so now whenever I see the big trees in the water meadows near the Rhine, I see uniformed airmen caught among the branches in a tangle of ropes and billowing parachutes, all of them soon to be gunned down by the soldiers who have been waiting for this moment.

Leendert was a gentle and friendly man with a slight limp: the after effects of Lyme disease. When I spent a lot of time here on holiday with my young family, we would have a nightly ritual of searching for the tiny black mark of a tick on the skin because they are especially numerous in the heathlands and woodlands, which are still littered with abandoned boulders deposited here at the end of the Ice Age. It turned out that as a schoolboy Leendert was taught by my ex-father-in-law, which added to the unexpected sense of familiarity. And then as we were sitting in the sunshine drinking coffee Sandra's younger sister happened to pass by and she stopped to chatter a greeting, making me feel as if I still belonged in a country where I no longer live.

Leendert explained that he is writing a book called *Where Do We Come From?*, beginning the human story three million years ago and ending it with the drowning of Doggerland, and with hardly any preamble, he launched into an explanation of hunter-gatherers and how they were different to us, the farmers who followed on their heels. He said that thanks to Adam and Eve, we inhabit a domestic world that places the natural world out of bounds. This separation was sustainable for a long while but now the pressure we are putting on the natural world has brought it to breaking point. Our arrogance is apparent even in the way that we call ourselves *sapiens,* implying that every other living creature is ignorant in comparison.

The Neanderthals, he said, also had fear and love and a creative imagination, but because we cannot grasp who they were with our limited understanding, we think of them as being less important. All the Stone Age cultures which contain the roots of who we have become are dismissed as some sort of dark age of ignorance.

As a student, Leendert studied physical geography. A colleague in the geology department was in contact with a group of Dutch fishermen who were pulling up bones in their trawling nets from a depth of some forty metres, close to the Brown Banks. There were huge bones from the Ice Age and even earlier but there were also much more recent bones: horse and beaver, deer and bear and the occasional, unmistakable, human artefact. The colleague was not interested in the younger bones or in barbed points carved from reindeer horn or bone and so Leendert took them over. They could all be dated at around 8,000 BC and the fact that many of them were what is called domestic and not hunting gear implied they were associated with human habitation, rather than being things lost on a hunt far from home. None of them had any sign of wear to indicate they had been carried by rivers or currents over many miles before they settled in this deep-water place and Leendert wanted to know why they were abandoned in the middle of the North Sea.

He said that by studying so many simple and yet beautiful worked tools and weapons over the years, you begin to see things: you see the mind of the people who made them and the landscapes they inhabited; the climate and vegetation and what animals were to be found living close by. He became aware of the sheer profusion of living creatures that belonged to this time and he spoke with a sort of nostalgia for such a world. He said what one learns from all such studies is not expertise but a gathering of uncertainties and it is from these uncertainties that one must work.

All hunter-gatherers lived so lightly on the earth and left few traces of their passing. The people of Doggerland seemed to produce very little in the way of decorative arts and even the scratched marks found on worked bones, stone and horn appear to be more like personal signatures of ownership rather than decoration for its own sake. With the start of the Holocene when the climate was warming up, it was possible for them to live in this rich environment all through the year, even though the sea levels were beginning to rise as much as two metres within a single century, making it necessary for them to learn to adapt to a land that was endlessly changing shape and size. He drew a little graph for me in my notebook to illustrate the sheer speed of what was happening. For him, the simple fact that these people were able to survive from one generation to the next was their greatest achievement.

He has spent much of his working life examining the delicate perfection of barbed hunting points; a broken twist of rope made from the bark of a tree that must have once been used as a basket for fish; a piece of wood that might have been a post in a dwelling; or human bones battered and broken by the events of a life and the circumstances of a death. He said you have to be rich in imagination when you try to do the work of understanding these people, while being careful to repress any fantasy. From their bones you can read of hunger and starvation, accidents and the effort of carrying heavy loads and you can work out that half of the children never reached the age of fourteen and very few adults were older than sixty. You can also see that many men and some women died as a result of violent conflict with other humans: there is often trauma to the skull, spear wounds piercing the chest or head. Usually burial sites will give an insight into a way of comprehending the world, but even the way the Mesoliths buried their dead is so complex and various it gives no clear understanding as to how these people comprehended the mystery and the reality of the world in which they found themselves.

When our conversation ended Leendert drove me to the station and we shook hands and kissed each other three times on the cheek, mainland Europe style. After I got back to Suffolk, he sent me a copy of a beautifully illustrated article he had written on Mesolithic barbed points and some eighty pages of his as yet unfinished book.

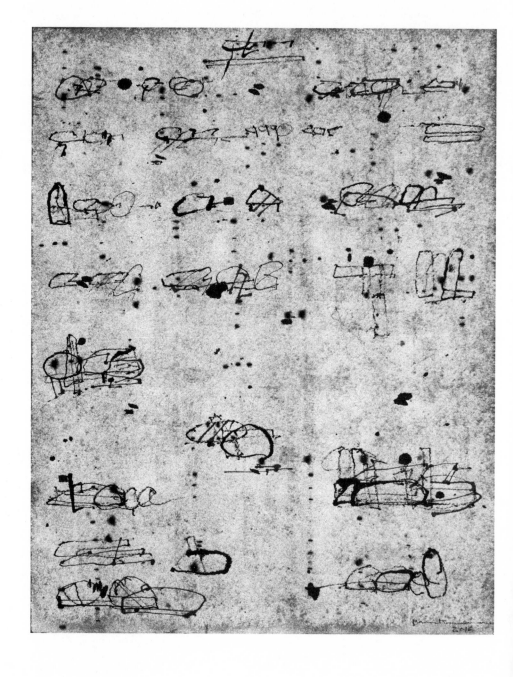

Time Song 10

There was once a lake.
It had been much bigger,
but for now
it was five kilometres long, two wide,
on the east coast of England
not far from the sea.
Sedge, reed and big-masted bullrush
along the water's edge,
willow and aspen further back,
then birch and clumps of hazel
on higher ground.

Roe deer, red deer,
and the last of the giant deer,
were here,
as well as lumbering elk
who like to browse with big lips
on underwater plants;
boar and beaver, otter and fox
even traces of two domesticated dogs,
one barely six months old.

Fish and amphibia including turtle
in the sweet rich water
and birds, lots of birds:
stork and crane patrolling the mud
and all that it contained;
divers and swimmers
testing the depths;
eagle and sea eagle,
hawk and falcon,
buzzard and harrier
in the sky by day,
owls by night.
And people
living their lives.

The creatures left nothing but bones
but the people left
the remains of sixteen wooden posts
from a dwelling that once stood in a circle;
a raised platform, purpose unknown;
a walkway along the water's edge;
part of a wooden paddle
to propel a boat forward on its quest;
beads of stone without a string to connect them;
arrows of stone without shaft or bow.
They also left:
bladelets and burins,
awls and adzes,

threaders and scrapers and stitchers;
delicately barbed points fashioned from red deer horn,
heavy mattock heads from elk antlers;
rolls of birch bark
which might have clothed the sides of their boats
or made tinder for fire
or glue for fixing things
one to the other.

Mysteriously
they kept several horns of red deer
attached to a patch of skull:
two holes bored into bone at the back
so it could be tied to the head of a man.

They must have gathered here
in spring and early summer.
Meeting with others of their kind
along the lake's edge.
Perhaps they hunted together,
exchanged goods and weapons,
wives, daughters and dogs,
stories, and laughter.
Perhaps a man danced,
deer horns sprouting from his head,
so by the light of the fire
he seemed both man and beast together.
Or perhaps men went hunting,

the deer looking up
and because of the horns
they saw only others of their kind
until death broke the spell.

After three hundred years,
the people moved elsewhere
and the lake diminished
until it was nothing but a few pools and bogs
holding fragments
of a forgotten story.

Based on *Early Humans* by Nick Ashton, Collins, 2017. I was going to go to Star Carr and then I decided not to because I was told there is no longer anything there to see, although I suppose I could have gone anyway since trying to see through the fact of absence is what this book is mostly about.

26

The island was originally a low hill on a plain close to the Severn River. The plain and the island were covered by a thick oak forest and because no other trees were represented, the oaks grew tall and straight, concentrating on the shared effort of reaching the light of the canopy. Around eight thousand years ago the plain was inundated by the sea; the trees died and stood as ghostly skeletons in the newly formed salt marsh and the hill became an island. For the next thousand years, as the sea levels rose further, the edges of the island were buried by salt-marsh silts and this is where the footsteps were found.

A group of people are here on the island. They will stay for a few days, weeks maybe, and then they will go somewhere else, but they will probably return, because this is a good place to be. They hunt for otter, deer, wild pig and aurochs and they use heated stones to help with cooking the flesh of larger creatures. They eat a lot of fish, especially eel, and they weave baskets and wattle fences made into V-shaped traps for funnelling and catching the retreating fish. They surely must eat birds, even though nothing has survived to prove it. And plants, of course, along with fruits and nuts, shellfish and whatever else belongs to a particular season. At night they might sleep under the shelter of small tepee-like structures made from branches, but the evidence is vague. For hunting and for butchering, they have tools fashioned from stone, wood and the antlers of deer and they abandon many of these tools when they leave.

Their children are often out on the estuary. They are barefoot. They step on creeping samphire and clumps of sea lavender, pushing through reeds and rushes and crossing open expanses of sand and the glutinous surface of river mud. Boys and girls. The oldest is perhaps fifteen, while the youngest can't be much more than three. Mostly they leave no trace of their passing, but sometimes the mud remembers them and holds the imprint of the pressure of toe and heel and instep. The feet tell who they are: their age, their height and weight, as well as the activity they were probably engaged in.

These children are not all here together as a group; they have run and walked and paused to stare or to make a decision, over a stretch of time that lasts from eight thousand to six thousand seven hundred years ago. Several of them were hunting, checking nets and traps, or gathering edible plants; others might simply have been playing. An older child carries a younger child on one hip; someone else slips on the mud.

Martin Bell has been involved in finding and interpreting the footprints since 2001. We met in the Waterstones café in Piccadilly; downstairs because the upstairs café was being used for a book launch. I was early – it seems to be part of my nature to be early and then to imagine that the person I am waiting for is late. Martin arrived on time. He brought a file of pictures and articles with him. One of the first things he said is how much he loves this work, which allows him to work in such beautiful and remote places.

Although I had read about the footprints and had seen photographs of them, I realised I still didn't understand how something so fragile could manage to survive for so long. Martin explained the process of preservation, illustrating his words with diagrams and photographs: a naked foot makes an impression in the fine clay-silt and then a big tide washes in and covers it with a thin layer of sand. This in turn is followed by more clay-silt, and more sand, until layer upon layer is built up. The

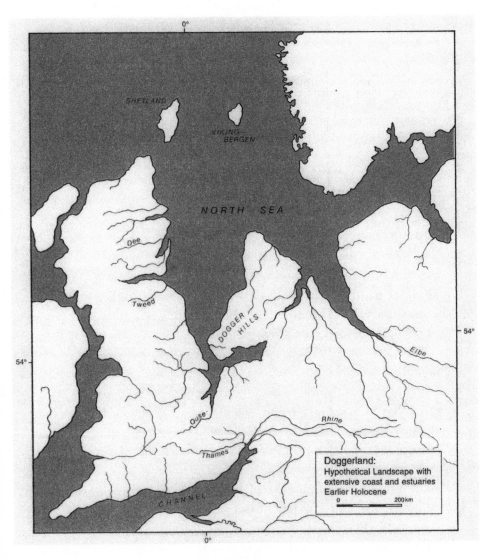

c. 10,000 BP

fine sand keeps a division between the layers of silt, holding the image safe, and as the depth of sediment increases, so it weighs down on what it lies upon, compressing it and causing the chemical changes that are the initial stages of fossilisation. These layers of sand and silt are known as laminations. You need to go through eleven metres of sediment to reach the Iron Age and then the Mesolithic lies some way beneath that.

The scattering of footprints are found on the lowermost foreshore of the estuary and are only likely to be exposed during the most favourable spring tides and then for less than two hours over a period of four to five days. As another complication: the sand and sediment are permanently on the move, so the most productive area that Martin and his colleagues were studying between 2001 to 2004 was suddenly engulfed by a sandbank up to three metres deep, which then remained on guard, as it were, for the next ten years. Recently it has been shifting and there is a good chance that work can start again quite soon.

The footsteps move between several campsites on the island that is now known as Goldcliff. There was a river about 230 metres wide, running to the east of the island, and it would have been a good place for hunting fish and birds and might have also provided an inland communication route by boat. A small amount of worked wood has been found close to the channel's edge, along with something which might be the remains of a basket used in fishing and part of a split plank and a small worked woodchip. There is evidence that people were here, however briefly, during all four seasons of the year.

In 2004, Rachel Scales, one of Martin's students at Reading University, developed a method of working with only the tips of her fingers, peeling back the thin layers of lamination inch by inch to reveal muddled patchworks of steps. After a month and towards the end of the time that was available before the spring tides closed in, a large chunk of mud fell away to reveal the most perfect footprint ever found: a child from seven thousand five hundred years ago, and every detail visible, the arch of the instep, the ball of the heel and the splayed toes with long sharp toenails. Twenty-four tracks of a solitary child, next to the tracks of a small unidentified bird, were found in an area four metres long and one metre wide. A little further on, a large bird, probably a crane, had made thirty-two careful steps over the mud and when Martin showed me a photograph I seemed to see its thin black legs and the peculiar, almost fastidious manner with which it lifts and then places each foot one in front of the next. On a deeper level of lamination and therefore of time, a heavy-bodied aurochs walked by.

On site H, Person 1 takes sixteen steps, walking from east to west and perhaps returning home to the island. He or she slides in the mud, and then hesitates when confronted with other human tracks. Persons 3, 4 and 5 are walking together and they seem to be moving with a common purpose; they pass the tracks of deer and perhaps they are out hunting. Persons 11 and 12 both struggle with their balance; they are only five or six years old and although they could be collecting fish that have been caught in nets, or gathering plants, they might simply be playing.

A wolf is patrolling the land, or perhaps it is one of the very early domesticated dogs; it is impossible to tell because only a single paw mark survives. Close by but on another level of time, a deer leaps into the air and when it lands it places its two narrow front hoofs in perfect symmetry, side by side.

Time Song 11

If they travel away
the people push their feet along the ground,
they place grass near the marks they have made.

Another man sees the grass and says,
'The people must have travelled to the water pool.'
And he goes to the water pool
seeking the people.

The people reverse branches.
They place the branch with the green top underneath,
the stump uppermost,
they draw their foot along the ground,
making a mark.

A man when he returns home
sees the branch and says,
'The people have reversed a branch
in the direction of the water hole.
I will go down to the water,
I will look for the people's footprints at the water,
at the place where they seem to have gone.'

He goes to the water,
he sees the people's footpath,
he takes it,
he follows it, follows it,
he finds them.

Based on *Specimens of Bushman Folklore* by Wilhelm Bleek and Lucy
Lloyd, London, 1911.

27

People walking. Their talk erupts like the babble of birds and then they return to the concentration of silence.

People pausing to look at the tracks of deer in the soft mud. They see the cloven cut of hoof and from that hieroglyph they see the animal in its entirety. They all see the same image.

They sit down to eat. They share the experience of biting and chewing, tasting and swallowing. They glance at each other and know that they share it.

They examine an object: the ankle bone from a horse that looks like a human torso; a twisted branch that could be mistaken for a snake; the pattern made by the excavation of beetles under the bark of a tree that seems to be a map of their own footprints when they walked on the mud beside the river. Such things tell them stories about who they are.

A person is holding something of value. A worked flint, perhaps. The person drops the object into the water, here, at this place, because this thing is important, it has power. The water receives the gift.

A man is preparing to go out hunting. In order to achieve the death of the animal that is to be hunted, he must become the animal. Inhabiting that other body is the first step towards possessing it. I feel my four sharp feet stepping through the rustle of grass. I feel the weight of horns upon my head. I feel an edge of pain as my heart is pierced by a stone point and I feel my blood running down the back of the man who has killed me, who is also myself, preparing to go out hunting.

A person dies. The breath has stopped. The body is naked and still. We put it on a heap of stones, or on an island separate from the mainland where we live. We might give it gifts, we might stroke it and say words to it, we might stare at it for a long time. But then we let it go. Days and nights. The weather is warm or cold. There are storms or stillness. The body's flesh is torn and eaten by animals, inhabited by insects. The bones become clean. They divide into segments. They are broken and scattered. They are part of everything that surrounds us.

Dreams are more real than the world itself. They take the dreamer to a place that can be entered, a place where I can speak with the dead and with living creatures that do not usually speak. If I want to change something or if I want to understand something that is already changing, then I need a dream to explain what is happening and what I must do, what all of us must do. A dreamer knows how to get to that other side, how to bring back information, so everyone can learn from it.

Sometimes, for a fleeting moment, I understand this. Sex can do it, when the boundary that separates me from another person is dissolved and I am as much him as I am myself.

There is the same overlap during pregnancy, when the creature that moves within my body is part of my body, part of who I am.

There were times with my husband who was dying and who knew he was dying and did not mind the fact of it even though he enjoyed being alive, there were times when he was right at the edge of his own mortality and I felt I was there beside him, seeing what he saw, the two of us filled with something like excitement, even though it meant we would be parted. We did once share a dream. I can't remember much about it, just that we had both been in exactly the same place and when we told each other it made us laugh like children.

172

28

1991 and I was in Australia, searching for whatever fragmented stories I could find about an Irish woman called Daisy Bates who had lived with the Pitjantjatjara people of the Great Western Desert for the last forty years of her long life. She died in 1954.

Someone mentioned Archie Barton to me. He was the leader of the Pitjantjatjara and was based in a town called Ceduna on the edge of the desert. He had met Daisy when he was a child and I was told that if anyone could put me in contact with others who had known her, he was the man. I was given his address and I wrote to him several times before I left England, but he never answered. I tried phoning, but that didn't work either.

I was with my first husband and our two young children and we were driving a camper van across the Nullarbor Plain. We stopped for a few days at Head of Bight, where sperm whales come to breed in the deep coastal waters. Every evening dingo dogs drew close to the camper and it seemed as though they would become tame and obedient if only I knew the language in which to call them. By day wallabies hid behind bushes, peeping out to gaze at us, their hunched backs giving the impression of shyness and apology. I found a wombat jawbone, speckled with bright yellow lichen that had still not dimmed its fierce colour, and I found a beautiful spiralling shell on the wide beach where there was no one apart from the solemn presences of three steep islands of rock that looked as if they were caught in the act of striding out into the sea. The rolling sand dunes were covered with sweeping traceries of movement made by the lizards and snakes we never saw. We ate bacon, eggs and beans on slices of white bread and swam naked.

And then on to Ceduna. The town was bleak. Huddles of Aborigines lay on the grass in a little park. Others were sitting hunched on the kerb of the one main street. The stink of alcohol which was also the stink of despair. I went up to one group and leant close and asked, 'Archie Barton? Where is Archie Barton?' Some of them shrugged and turned away, but one or two said, 'He here somewhere. He sit down in him house. You find him, him house.' They pointed towards a street and bit by bit we got to where we wanted to go.

I rang the bell and a young woman opened the door. 'They here!' she said, as if we were late for our appointment. She led us into a plain room with a big table and a shiny embroidered picture of a waterfall on the wall, alongside the famous print of the blue-faced lady looking sad in a kimono which used to be for sale in Boots the Chemist.

We were invited to sit down and Archie Barton arrived. His daughter, who had let us in, brought mugs of sweet and milky orange tea and he took his tea and sat opposite me and stared at me for maybe ten minutes or more saying nothing. I didn't feel in any way threatened by the staring; it seemed like a conversation without words.

Then he said, 'You go to the desert tomorrow. Denis take you. Meet the old people. Tonight you sleep here in the yard. Up early.'

With our plans settled he began to tell me about Daisy Bates, who had hidden him in a cupboard when the whites came to kidnap him and put him in an orphanage. As he spoke he was back in the cupboard and overwhelmed by fear. The whites did not find him but they came again and now they seized him tight and his mother cried with despair and he cried to see himself snatched from her, the tears returning to his eyes as he felt himself being carried away from her and from the land of his birth.

I am not sure how the transition was made, but now Archie Barton was talking about those islands of rock at Head of Bight and how they had been three young men running from some danger in the Dreamtime and now he was watching the story of the creation of the world as if it was happening in this present moment and as he spoke he held my eyes in his own so that what he said played out before me like scenes in a film.

The next morning we went into the desert, following Denis who drove very fast. The corrugated surface of the sandy track made speaking impossible and all our cooking pans fell on to the floor of the camper and jumped and rattled as if they had come alive and were in a lot of trouble.

We were on our way to the Ooldea Soak, which was where Daisy Bates had set up camp. For many thousands of years it had been an oasis within the desert, an underground lake sealed within a capsule of clay but seeping some of its moisture to the surface, so that water could always be found here. But then in the late 1940s, the East West Railway Line was built from Adelaide to Perth, and the men broke through the clay in their eagerness to feed water to their trains. And that was that, the soak was emptied and nothing was left of it apart from a single struggling fig tree and a broken water pipe.

A group of old people were there, sitting around, talking softly to each other, their voices like birdsong. No alcohol, but everyone had that same inward look of sadness that you see in the photos of the San, of the Innu, the Netsilik, the people of the Dene Nation. All of them staring towards what it is that has gone.

175

Feather-light handshakes from dry hands. Eyes searching my face to read what sort of a person I might be. A man pointed to the fig tree and said, 'Thou shall not steal!' and laughed as he made the gesture of someone beating him with a stick.

I was drawn to a woman called May and when she climbed one of the red hills of sand I followed her and sat beside her. She stared at her surroundings and said, 'Daisy Bates look this way and she say, "Ah, nice!" Daisy Bates she look that way and she say, "Ah, nice!"' and she gestured with her eyes, drinking in the land that filled her with its emptiness and its colour.

Later, before we parted, May and another woman showed me where Daisy's tent had stood and they gazed at the place of its absence as if they were wondering if they should call to her and then perhaps she might answer. May picked up a thin glass bottle, its surface mottled like a butterfly's wing. 'Daisy Bates' lemonade,' she said and gave it to me. And then within a space of a few minutes the two of them searched the empty sand and found three flint spearheads, a piece of stone decorated with little scratch marks and a hole drilled into it so it could be hung around the neck, and a meteorite, black and shiny and no bigger than a pea, but bursting with energy. They gave me their gifts, smiling with pleasure as I received them.

Time Song 12

We feel in our bodies when certain things are going to happen;
it is a kind of tapping of the flesh, which tells us things.
A man who feels his body move in this way
orders the others to be silent,
and the man himself must be altogether still
when he feels that his body is tapping inside.
Those who disobey the tapping of the flesh
get killed, or something else happens to them.

The tapping of the flesh tells us which way not to go,
which arrow not to use,
it also warns us when people are coming,
making it possible to perceive these people we are searching for.

If a woman who has gone away is returning to her home,
the man who is sitting there
feels on his shoulders
the thong with which the woman's child
is slung over her shoulders;
he feels the tapping there.

If a man who is being searched for has an old wound,
the one who is searching feels a tapping at the wound's place,

he feels when the man he is searching for is walking.
He says to his children,
'Look for Grandfather, for Grandfather seems to be coming
and that is why I feel the place of his body's old wound.'

The children look.
They say to their father, 'A man is coming.'
Their father says, 'He was the one I felt coming
at the place of his old wound.'

Based on *Specimens of Bushman Folklore* by Wilhelm Bleek and Lucy Lloyd, London, 1911.

29

I am standing on the northern coastline of Doggerland. I look out across
a sheltered bay scattered with little islands. A thin column of smoke
rises into the air from one of the islands which is close to the land's
edge and also close to a deep channel cut by a river into the shallow
sea. A line of fish traps woven from willow has been fixed along the
edge of the channel.

The people who are here are good at surviving. They navigate
their narrow canoes through the inland waterways. They sleep within
the protection of an island or on wooden platforms built out over the
water of a lake or a lagoon. They build wooden walkways for crossing
the marshes and the swamps. They know how to follow the movement
of the seasons and the migrations of birds, fish and animals and they
do their best to adapt to the transformations of the land and the water.
But the world they inhabit is in a state of flux; sea levels are rising
at a speed that can be seen from one generation to the next, so
everyone has the vivid recollection of what has been lost and the fear
of what is happening and about to happen.

The people could try to escape by moving further inland, but such
a move is not simple. The coastal areas provide the richest hunting
grounds and they hold the stories that root this particular community
into itself and its own sense of belonging. The bones of their dead are
somewhere nearby and the dead do not like being abandoned.

So they hold on, even though the land they inhabit is becoming
altered and strange. Trees that had once been part of a forest are now
like a nervous crowd of black skeletons, the salt water sloshing around

their roots. The inundation of the sea keeps breaking through the natural barriers of the land, so that shelters and hearths, fishing nets and weirs, food stores prepared against the coming winter, oyster beds and the sites where birds' eggs can be gathered, everything is in danger of being swept away or covered over. Each time the salt waters claim a new expanse of territory the air is made thick with the stink of drowned carcasses and rotting vegetation.

The people must do something to calm the rising sea and to limit its anger. They offer gifts in little clustered depositions like the words of a prayer. At the site known as Hoogevaart in Holland a carefully placed collection of beautifully worked flints and aurochs skulls were found and a similar gathering of bones and stone adzes, cutting implements, spearheads and maceheads have been uncovered in other areas where the waters were rising. In Norway, Denmark, Holland, Scotland and elsewhere treasured objects were set down apparently to mark the dangerously shifting border between two elements that are as different to each other as life is from death.

The flooding of the land sped up dramatically around eight thousand years ago, with an event known as the Storegga Slide, the word *storegga* coming from the Old Norse and meaning 'Great Edge'. Because of the rising temperature, the thick glacial sediment laid down beneath the sea ice had become increasingly unstable, triggering a submarine landslide in which some one thousand miles of an underwater cliff collapsed close to the coast of Norway. The force of this collapse created a tsunami that travelled northward and eastward. Across the gentle undulations of Doggerland, this wave did not come crashing down, but it caused a vast flood to swoop over the land, swirling around hills and islands.

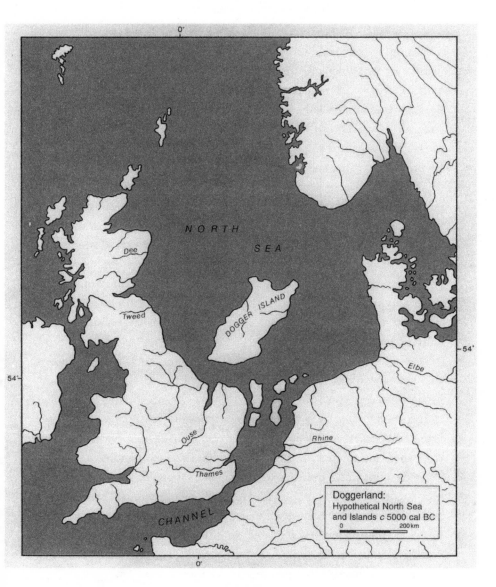

Doggerland:
Hypothetical North Sea
and Islands *c* 5000 cal BC
0   200km

c. 7,000 BP

Time passes backwards as well as forwards and I find myself wondering what happened in the past with the same urgent uncertainty with which I wonder what might be approaching in the future. It could be that the hunter-gatherers abandon their diminishing and broken territories for ever, but it's also possible they find a way to go on living in the remnants of Doggerland for several more generations. I wrote to Bryony, asking what she thought, and she replied, 'I still think there was something of Doggerland surviving after the Storegga Slide and the tsunami. What is lacking is evidence . . . and I find there are more new questions than answers . . . So I think you are free to speculate.'

I wrote to Leendert and he said, 'Sea levels were around twenty-five metres below our present levels . . . But this was a one-time event, *not* an acceleration of the gradual inundation. Dramatic for the people living there and in the lowlands around the initial North Sea, but people will have returned and resettled the areas, just as we see nowadays after tsunami catastrophes.'

A couple of weeks ago I was at Covehithe. The bank that divides the coastal path from the sand on the beach had been swept away in the week since I was last there and a whole length of cliff had tumbled to the shore faster than I ever thought possible. An inland sweetwater lake had been breached and the water was pouring out of it in a rushing river, too wide to cross. A great dirty tongue of sand had been swept in over the dunes and into the reedbeds and I have never seen quite so much modern rubbish: plastic fuel tanks – one of them still regurgitating its stinking liquid – shoes, the linings of sanitary towels, lengths of rope, pieces of polystyrene and a mishmash of broken objects whose purpose could no longer be identified. The thin trees crowding along the edge of the cliff seemed to be queuing up for their execution.

But then yesterday, when I was on the same beach, it looked fresh and beautiful from the last sweep of the tide. The sweetwater lake was again intact and calm and noisy with birds. I walked among some tumbled chunks of sand and earth and came across a young seal lying comfortably in the sunshine. I crouched beside it and talked to it and it responded to my voice by wriggling like a puppy and flapping its flippers together to make a soft clapping noise. I talked some more and it raised its head to gaze at me, one creature encountering another.

I remained in its gentle company for twenty minutes or more and then I made my way back to where I had parked the car. If I'd gone on walking along the coast in a northerly direction for another hour or so, I'd have reached the place where Bob Mutch found the stash of flints that proved human beings had been here more than seven hundred thousand years ago. Some twelve miles on and I'd pass what is left of the mouth of the Yare, which the Romans defended with their fortress towers. Another twenty miles and I'd come to Happisburgh, where the fossilised footsteps of an earlier people were seen and quickly recorded on the beach. Twelve more miles and I'd reach the bank of an extinct river where Jonathan found the jaw of a rhinoceros in the old mud. Continuing around the Wash and up into Lincolnshire and Yorkshire, I'd eventually reach the site of the Mesolithic settlement of Star Carr, built to straddle the waters of a lake that had been close to the old coastline of Doggerland in the days before that coastline vanished.

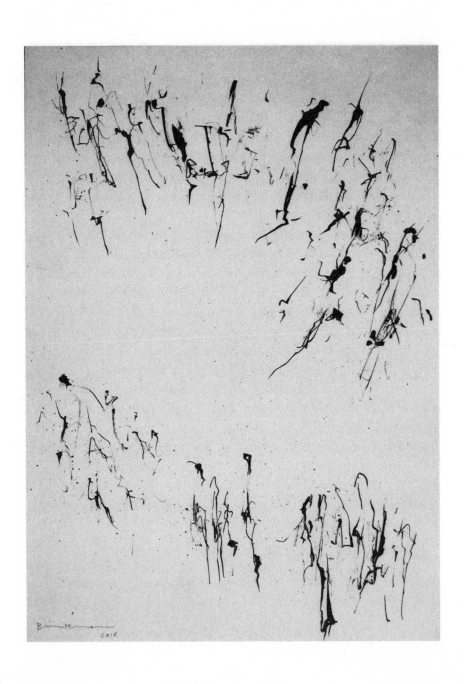

Time Song 13

Evidence of late Mesolithic
defensive wooden structures
have been found
scattered around Doggerland's edges.
Their function is unclear;
perhaps they were built
to keep human enemies at bay.
Perhaps they were facing
that other enemy:
the rising waters.

The land was diminishing,
imbued with dread,
marshy and salt-sodden:
spring without the celebration
of the increase of life,
summer and autumn without the certainty
of growing fat and fruitful,
winter as the possibility
of an end to everything.

People began to die more often
from acts of violence to each other,

the skeletons of men in particular
showing fatal damage from heavy blows
to the left-hand side of the skull,
right femurs broken through
from parrying those blows.
You see how a stone-tipped spear
raced through the barricade of ribs
to lodge itself
close to the site of the heart
it pierced.

The bodies of women
lie beside their men,
eloquent in their silence;
a child might lie between them,
the small bones
often marked
by hunger's delicate traces.

Based on a visit to the Vedbaek Museum and the battlefield of
Skanderborg, in Alken, Denmark.

30

My husband began to die in the garden. He settled himself down on a bank of flowers under the canopy of an oak tree and something happened within his brain so that the person who he was ceased to be, even though his eyelids fluttered and his heart was still beating. A flashing ambulance took him to hospital. He was placed in a narrow bed in a little room and I sat beside him and witnessed his departure. No sign of any pain, no movement apart from the slight lifting of one hand. A nurse came in every hour or so to check that everything was all right – as all right as it could be.

The occasion, if that is the word, was serious rather than sad. It was the seriousness of a kind of music when a single instrument is playing; the seriousness of the sky as it turns black before a thunderstorm; the seriousness of the last days of a pregnancy when you know that whatever happens the baby must emerge into the air, because you cannot hold its vastness in your belly any longer.

And then he was gone and the balance was tipped, making his absence greater than his presence. I became aware of the details of him: his ears, his hair, his nose, the beauty of his hands and feet. When I got home that night I went out into the meadows behind this house. The moon was full. I walked for an hour or so through a land in which everything – trees and bushes and grass – was clearly visible and yet without colour or substance.

I think my two children arrived the following morning and then his daughter came from Amsterdam the next day, or perhaps it was the day after, I'm not sure. We all went to see him. We were led into a waiting room with bright daylight pouring in through the window, soft chairs, a box of paper hankies and an aquarium holding the darting activity of tropical fish, including a little shoal of neons, each one carrying a flash of electric blue along its sides. The mortuary next door was so dimly lit it was almost dark and there was the corpse wrapped in a sheet, eyes closed and a face that looked as impassive as stone. We all said our farewells and his daughter asked the nurse who was with us if we might have a curl of his hair. The nurse did not seem surprised by the request. He went and fetched scissors and four little velvet pouches such as you might use to hold a ring, and my husband's daughter cut four locks of her father's hair and the nurse tied them with thread and put one lock in each pouch. I have mine now in a drawer which also holds my passport, along with certificates of marriage and divorce, birth and death.

There is no way of knowing how the people of Doggerland dealt with the act of dying in all the many forms it can take, but once the act was completed, they needed to dispose of the body. This is a time in which every aspect of the natural world is alive; even stones and the wind have their own voice and vitality and will listen if they are spoken to. A hunter has to understand what it is to be the animal he wishes to kill and that animal has to agree to be killed, enabling the hunter and his family to live. The gift of death in exchange for the gift of life. The hunter butchers the animal, stripping the skin from the carcass, cutting away the meat, parting the joints one from the other, smashing the bones to reach the marrow.

This process can be made to work the other way round when the body of a dead person is put in a place where animals do the butchery; they remove the innards, tear at the flesh and devour everything they can eat, leaving the stripped carcass for maggots and insects to finish the work. Or the corpse was cut and stripped and broken into pieces by people using tools for their work and these disarticulated bones were allowed to follow their own process, at the mercy of animals and the weather. The gift of death in exchange for the gift of life, and what eventually remains might be gathered up and put somewhere or simply scattered on the ground without ceremony.

Fragments of human bones have been found in middens, those huge Mesolithic refuse heaps which often contain tens of thousands of items: the shells of limpets and hazelnuts alongside the bones of fish and animals, men, women and children, all of them rattling together in the proximity to which they belong. It could seem like casual abandonment; but in one of the middens on Oronsay in the Western Isles of Scotland, the remains of a human hand had been carefully reassembled and placed on the flipper of a seal. There is no way of knowing the meaning of such a gesture, but that does not destroy its power.

Take it a step further. If you are part of the natural world, absorbed into it as a tree is absorbed into the earth that holds its roots, as a bird is absorbed into the migratory pattern of the year, then it follows that death is not a final ending, it is just one of the many stages of your belonging. The dead are there in the places they knew, the places they inhabited and moved through and their presence speaks to the living.

Human corpses were also left intact and lowered into a fissure in the ground; they were buried on islands used just for that purpose, or placed in a cave, or in the sea, or a peat bog, or some other natural tomb.

The remains of the dead were often accompanied by fine gifts and sometimes the most perfect axeheads and other valued objects were intentionally broken, split in half with one blow, before being handed over to the other side as a mark of respect or of memory.

31

19 June 2017 and the sky is as blue as any image of heaven and there's not a breath of wind and I've just been told it's hotter today in England than it is in Madagascar. Two months ago I was in Denmark making a radio programme with my friend Tim Dee. We flew to Copenhagen and then drove to Jutland along flat motorways of which I remember nothing apart from the orange juice we bought in a motorway café which had transparent floating bits in it that must have been made out of jelly. For the radio programme we went to see Tollund Man and other bog bodies within the museum caskets that hold them and we visited the old peat bogs from which they had been lifted.

On our way back to Copenhagen we stopped at the Vedbaek Museum which houses the contents of a Mesolithic burial site found by accident in 1975, when the foundations for a new village school were being dug in some rough land on the edge of a fjord. Seventeen graves, containing the remains of twenty-two people, all of them dating from nine thousand years ago.

The museum was opened in 1980 and it's a sort of annexe to the main Søllerød museum which specialises in modern art. When we came in and asked to buy tickets, the young woman at the desk thought we had made a mistake, surely we had come to see the Rauschenberg exhibition. She was thin and angular and shy and bold all at once and she made me think of a learner driver who lurches the car forward and then stalls it with equal suddenness. She gave a little shriek of delight when we said we really had come for the burials.

The building comprised three little rooms following on from each other and the displays were simple and without any special effects. The first glass cabinet contained a branch to represent *a place in the forest where a squirrel jumps from a tree top in flight from the lightning-fast bite of the pine marten* and the jumping squirrel and the lunging pine marten both looked weary and a bit motheaten from holding the pose for so long. Then there was the shell of a swamp turtle found in a swamp, the bark from a linden tree, a capercaillie with the black fan of its tail feathers raised for a courtship dance, and a great auk which, as the notice explained, had been reconstructed from the bodies of eleven razorbills.

The next cabinet contained the complete skeleton of a dog. The legs were bent as if the animal was still in pursuit of the prey it would dutifully bring back to the hunter and the body was honoured with a scattering of ochre the colour of dried blood.

And now to the people. We saw the skeleton of a woman who was estimated to be in her fifties and thus very old. Her head lay on a pillow of whitened deer antlers that sprouted out around her skull as if she was wearing them as a great bleached crown. Even though her skull was thrown back into a look of macabre laughter, there was a tremendous dignity about her, the sense that she was a person of importance, a person who demanded respect. Then there was a man who had been killed by an axe blow to his head and the stone axe was next to his shattered skull, telling the story of what had happened. A woman lay beside him and their young child was between them, the bones of the three bodies touching each other as if for comfort. The long thin feet of the adults were like the feet of wading birds.

But the one who impressed me most was a woman who had been buried with her newborn baby. You saw the tenderness of the two of them lying there together and from the way they had been so carefully placed you could feel that their death had caused much sorrow. She was young, not yet twenty. Her head had been covered by a leather cap decorated with perforated deer teeth and snail shells, but the leather had vanished and all that was left was a scattering of teeth and shell. Her tiny baby was at her right side and her right hand was turned so that her fingers were cupped protectively beneath his feet. His ribs were partly broken and splayed out in a configuration that made them look like a butterfly. A flint knife blade had been placed on his belly, maybe to indicate the hunting he would have done, had he lived to be a man.

What makes you pause and catch your breath, bringing the prickling of tears to your eyes, is the fact that the baby had been placed on the outstretched wing of a swan. The bones of the arch of the upper part of the wing seem to be growing directly out of the woman's shoulder and although the white feathers vanished long ago, it is not difficult to imagine them softly cradling the little body. I could almost hear the creak of the wing as the bird lifted the child up from its grave and into the element of air.

My husband's coffin was made of strong cardboard. It had nylon rope handles and it was lined with white synthetic satin fitted over pieces of foam rubber to serve as a sort of nest for the deceased. I thought it would be nice to paint it and so it was brought to the house and put on the floor next to the sofa. My friend Jayne came to help me and the task was curiously convivial. I got a pot of red ochre powder paint from the studio and mixed it with water and Jayne suggested adding a bit of polyurethane glue to give it more hold. The same with cobalt blue. I drew the outline of a simple range of mountains, because my husband loved mountains, and Jayne and I coloured them in, as children might. Behind the mountains we painted the brightness of a blue sky and a tiny splash of blue fell on the wooden floor and is still there almost four years later, holding on tight.

Two representatives of the funeral company arrived to take the coffin away: a young man and a young woman dressed in black with white shirts and white cotton gloves, and when they entered the house they kept their heads tilted down as a sign of the seriousness of the occasion and walked with slow bobbing steps which made them look all the more like penguins. They took it in turn to speak, their words trailing off into awkward pauses. 'Oh! Isn't that lovely!' the woman said when she saw the painted coffin and that made the man looked startled and ashamed as if she had blasphemed or farted, so then she blushed with confusion and clasped her gloved hands together in a vow of silence. They stood and hovered around for a while and rejected the offer of a cup of tea and then they carried the empty coffin to the black hearse that was parked outside.

This was to be a cremation: no preacher to explain the fact of death and no tried and tested ritual to guide us through the ceremony. I had found a piece of ivy that had grown its clinging arms into a rough circle around the trunk of a hawthorn in the meadow and I decorated it with flowers from the garden and people added more flowers, making it like a wreath to put on the coffin. Friends added a branch from an olive tree and I balanced my husband's favourite hat among the clusters of black fruit and the elegance of the pale leaves. Another friend placed an apple next to the branch and I imagined how it would explode softly in the flames.

The sun was shining. We carried the coffin into a room filled with chairs. Someone gave a short speech, our children spoke, I said something. We had three pieces of music: a composition by Steve Reich that sounded like yelping angels; Lester Young puff-puffing his way through the happy-sadness of 'On the Sunny Side of the Street'; and then came Blind Willie Johnson who was born the descendant of slaves in the cotton state of Texas in 1897. In a gravelly voice that seemed to come from a long way off, he asked the question,

> *Won't somebody tell me,*
> *Answer if you can!*
> *Want somebody tell me,*
> *What is the soul of a man?*

A couple of weeks after the cremation, the ashes were ready to be collected. They were in a murky-red plastic container with a screw-top lid, my husband's name and death date printed on to a white label. The container was surprisingly heavy. When I got home I unscrewed the lid and looked inside. The ashes were in a clear plastic bag. I lifted out the bag and opened it. No sign of bits of bone, just a heap of rather industrial grey powder that could have been ground concrete. That evening I put a sprinkling of my husband's remains into a bowl of yoghurt and honey and ate it, startled by the act and by the grittiness in my mouth.

32

When I was twenty I wrote a book called *How the World As We Know It Today Began.* I made it in a little flimsy notebook, postcard size, with a watercolour illustration on the right-hand page and a text typed out on my Olivetti 22 and stuck in place on the left.

This was the story of Adam and Eve in the walled garden of Paradise and it was quite conventional in structure, although God did keep saying that everything was good but not good enough and there was no apple, just a whispering snake. The sin was the sexual act which the first couple committed three times, three positions on three consecutive pages with big smiles on their faces while the angel looked on in dismay.

I considered it to be a serious book, or at least almost serious. I was interested in the idea of the enclosed bubble of being happy for ever, at ease with God and nature, and I was interested in how a simple physical act could irredeemably destroy such contentment and throw poor old Adam and Eve into the confusions of a much harsher and antagonistic world in which they had to struggle to stay alive.

I made some more picture books, including one called *An Alphabet of People,* and that also had pictures on one side, facing a short verse for each rather tragic individual and their alphabetically listed fears. Each verse ended with the refrain: *oh Homo, Homo sapiens!*

I eventually gathered up courage and took my books to the owner of a small printing press. He was welcoming but a bit over-solicitous in his manner. He gazed at the naked people and their fears and at Adam and Eve and their sin and with a deep sigh he patted me on the shoulder and said it was a psychiatrist I should be talking to, not a publisher. He asked if I would like to have lunch with him. I declined his offer and went on my way.

I moved to Majorca where I started working with a very academic American woman on a project we called *Beyond Genesis,* although I was not at all sure about the title. This was to be a collection of myths that had their origin in the story of Paradise and its loss, collected from all sorts of different cultures and historical times, just so long as the first man was Adam and the first woman was Eve. We had the Cathars in fourteeth-century France, the Bogomils in tenth-century Bulgaria, the Yezidis of Iraq and some rather haphazardly converted Aborigines in Australia whose Fall was engineered by an angry and racist God and He sent them to live in Devil-Devil Land which was the desert landscape that had been their home for many thousands of years.

The manuscript for that project grew increasingly fat and heavy, until the day when I began the opening of a new chapter with the words: *Civilisation has always.* I felt a cold shock of surprise as I realised I had no idea of what civilisation had always done, or if it had always done anything, and so the book came to an abrupt end.

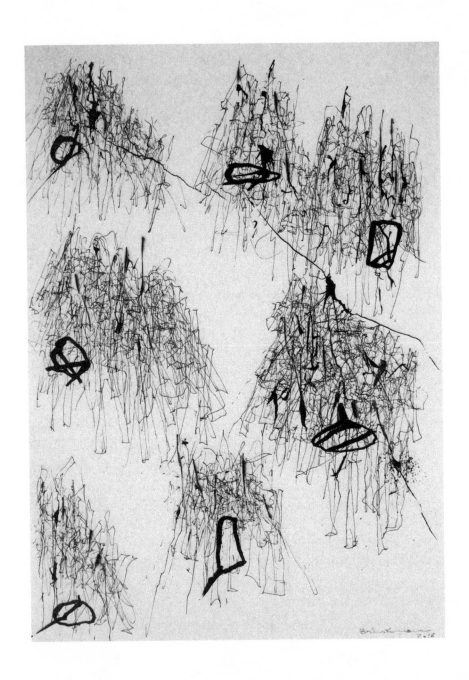

Time Song 14

Next week I will be sixty-nine,
the years for the living
moving on as they do
without ever pausing.

I have been busy with this book for quite a while,
and it often seems
the longer I work on it
the shorter it becomes.

Now the Mesolithic is more or less over
while the Neolithic
in which we more or less still are
begins.

The Neolithic means
owning things:
property, money,
wives and cattle
and whatever else
is worth fighting for,
to the death,
if need be.

The first steps of the Neolithic
were taken some eight thousand years ago
in the land of milk and honey
(now the land of oil and war).
The softening climate
provided food
for everyone;
no need to wander
or struggle,
plenty of time to sit still
and grow fat.

But sitting still
brought changes in its wake:
human numbers grew,
crops failed,
the people as hungry
as they were numerous.
The close proximity to domestic animals
led to sickness and epidemics:
dirty water,
fleas in the bed,
rats in the barns,
heaps of excrement
From man and beast,
on all sides.

War and catastrophe
entered stage right,
the seven apocalyptic horses
on the gallop,
nostrils flaring.
'What have we done?'
the people asked their god
and from out of the silence
their god seemed to say
they had sinned
and deserved punishment.

Many of them left their homes,
travelling north and east
like a conquering army
in search of more land
for crops and cattle,
more women as child bearers,
more places to claim as their own.
The hunters and gatherers
were swept along or swept away
by this tide of change
which is how – to put it simply –
the Mesolithic came to an end,
and the Neolithic took over;

turning the techniques of hunting
into the technology of warfare.

Based on *The Good Book of Human Nature: An Evolutionary Reading of the Bible* by Carel van Schaik and Kai Michel, Basic Books, 2016.

Part Three

No Time at All

What falls away is always. And is near.

THEODORE ROETHKE, 'The Waking'

33

14 August 2017 and a wren is in the house. It keeps hurling its little body against the high panes of glass that cannot be opened just above an open door and an open window. It's a surreal variation of the story told by the Venerable Bede, in which it is a cold and stormy night and the King and his people are feasting in the firelit warmth of a Great Hall when a sparrow flies like an arrow through one end of the building and out again at the other end. He says the bird within the hall is like our experience of life, while the darkness beyond the hall is the uncharted territory from which we emerge and into which we must return. But my wren, if I can call it that, is trapped and cannot escape, even though escape would be so easy.

It's almost midday. The sky is white and without substance. The air is cold and still. In Southern Europe people are deep in a heatwave.

I finished a time song this morning. Perhaps I finished it too quickly, but I had been trying to write it for ages so that should make for a balance.

In order to continue I hold the image of a leaf in my mind. Someone told me of finding an aspen leaf deep in a peat bog and the leaf emerged as perfect and fresh as the moment in autumn when it dropped from the branch of the tree that held it, and settled on the surface of clear brown water and sank down and lay there unchanged for more than a thousand years. And then as it is exposed to the air, the leaf in the hand of the person who has picked it up turns pale and disintegrates and ceases to be.

The wren must have knocked itself out on the glass. I heard a tiny thud as it fell to the floor. I lifted it up as light as a butterfly and it opened one eye to stare at me morosely. I took it into the garden and placed it among the leaves and flowers of a pot of blue lobelia and eventually it gathered enough energy to fly away.

34

The blackened stumps are from trees that once grew in Doggerland. They are mostly oak and some of them once stood at a height of fifteen metres. As soon as they emerge from under the sand or clay that covers them and into the air, they begin to disintegrate.

I was again staying with my friend Jayne and we planned to go to the coastal village of Holme-next-the-Sea, where you are most likely to see the Mesolithic forest bed, if it is there to be seen. It's also the place which erupted into the public imagination when a circle of tree stumps surrounding a central altar or burial platform was revealed during a very low tide. The platform was made from the base of a tree, planted upside down so that its spread roots could cradle something the size of a human body. Other such circles had been revealed before, but someone gave this one the name Seahenge, which, with its echo of Stonehenge, brought great flurries of visitors to behold the miracle of the past borne into the present.

It was not long before the decision was made that the tree stumps must be removed to protect both them and the area from damage and so they were lifted out of the sands and taken to soak in a bath of chemicals, until they were strong enough to be put on show in a local museum. The place where they had stood was marked with a pole that can be seen when the tide is really low.

This was a luminous morning with a blue sky that looked as thin and clear as glass; the air was warm, in a spring that has hardly known any warmth. We parked in the main car park and walked to the visitor centre. There were lots of noticeboards carrying pictures of the henge and the coast and its birds, somehow ensuring that the real world with its distances and absences and fuzzy outlines was bound to be a disappointment. The visitor centre café was closed but a woman raced out of the building and said we were parked in the wrong car park which did and did not matter and she was going on holiday the following morning and she really needed the holiday and had only just started to pack and her partner hadn't even got that far, he was the warden, he was overseeing the cutting down of the pine trees that had been killed by the storm surge of November 2013. It was the trees on the lower ground that had died, their roots standing in the salty water, and now it was thought their branches might fall and hurt a member of the public. She said she knew nothing about the Seahenge and it was a nightmare until they took it away; we should talk to her partner, he was wearing a puffa jacket, he knew everything, he'd lived at Holme since the late 1980s.

We followed a track that led through the pines, the sound of chainsaws getting louder. We spoke to a young man in a fluorescent jacket and a plastic helmet whose job was to make sure that nobody got close to the dead trees that might drop their branches. He also knew nothing about the submerged forest. He had done a degree in zoology, studying pigs and how they responded to more humane treatment, but unfortunately the pigs he was studying kept getting slaughtered and so it was not easy to come to any conclusions. I asked him what sort of work he would like to be doing and he grinned and said paid work would be nice.

We crossed the delicate border between the sand dunes where the trees grew and the coast where nothing grew. The tide was still quite high, and the beach looked as though it had been newly laid out: a great thick layer of pale sand dumped on whatever was hidden beneath.

The sand made a seamless connection with the gentle pull and push of the sea's edge, but apart from that the sea hardly moved. The blue sky went darker towards the horizon, where those two elements fused. I thought of what Bryony had said about the people who used to live in places like this, one foot on the land and one in the water.

We started walking towards Hunstanton where the uppermost bulge of East Anglia turns a sharp corner and sweeps back into the Wash. A soft wind. Every stone and pebble, every shell and dried wisp of seaweed had its own shadow attached to it, giving even the tiniest things a sort of power and dignity.

As the tide pulled back, the wading birds came. Oystercatchers, hopping as if they only had the one foot to stand on and then launching out together in a perfect formation only inches above the land, their sharp cries like the sound of regret.

A fair number of cormorants were airing their wings; some had white patches on their rumps which is something to do with the breeding season being close and others had the white bibs of juveniles. When they fly, necks outstretched and bodies as determined as a weapon, they seem so ancient, as if they are still connected to their reptile relatives. I looked them up when I got home and although they weren't flying around in the company of pterodactyls and giant dragonflies, they were present in the warmer interglacials of the Ice Age, as far back as the Middle Pleistocene which means at least a couple of million years.

And then all the bobbing and skittering shore birds whose names I tend to muddle up: sandpipers and sanderlings, dunlin, little stints and turnstones and a redshank or perhaps it was a greenshank.

We drifted a bit inland in the almost too bright sunshine to where a channel of saltwater had looped its way in from the sea, so that eventually it would encircle and cut off a whole chunk of the fragile coast. The nearside bank of this channel was bounded by the palest and finest sand. The wind rippled the clear water, making it seem as if it was a flowing river but in a different world than our own, and I was back with thoughts of the dead and how close they can seem, even though they are utterly beyond reach.

We walked on. I picked up a piece of chalk honeycombed with the pinpricks of some sort of tiny boring animal. I found a strange and rather sinister object, almost soft and almost white, with the look of drowned human flesh. I vaguely knew what it was, but I couldn't catch it in my memory.

In Hunstanton we stopped in a hotel bar, sitting outside in a curious corral of varnished pine wood and protected from the wind by glass barriers; it was rather like being an animal from another country, held in the compound of a safari park. We ordered cheese and pickle sandwiches on white bread, as soft and odd as that white and fleshy sea thing, and a man wearing a black and shiny leather trilby tilted back to reveal the vastness of his forehead walked past, led by a piebald bull terrier straining at the lead. There was a look of menace in the man, maybe because of the way the dog pulled him forward, or because the hat looked as if it was part of a fascist uniform. And then he said something to the woman who had gone ahead of him and he had a funny squeaky voice which made him seem all the more aggressive, as if he was bound to be angry, having to live with the odd vulnerability of the sound he produced.

On the way back to the car park we met Puffa Jacket. 'The drowned forest has gone,' he said, 'and goodness knows when it will next appear. All you can see for now are those lumps of black peat that get washed up along the shore and they contain bits of the roots of trees, scraps of grass or marshland, alongside seashells and the holes made by piddocks. The trees disintegrate first and then the peat their roots were standing in breaks away and is carried along the beach.' He explained that under the peat there is a layer of clay from river silt and under the clay there is another drowned forest. He looked surprised when he said this, even though I am sure he has said it many times.

He said Seahenge was a disaster for this area. The clever journalist who thought up the name wrote an article about the mysterious circle of tree trunks with an upside-down trunk at the centre of the circle, with photographs to show how it looked. That led to more photos and articles and suddenly seventeen thousand visitors from all corners of the world, and especially from Japan, began to turn up in busloads. Druids and others who believed in the old gods came to claim the henge as their birthright, demanding it be left where it was so they could worship it. There was quite a bit of aggression and all this in a nature reserve that would never expect more than a couple of hundred visitors on a good day in the summer. 'It's nothing but a circle of wooden poles surrounding an upside-down trunk for carrying a dead body,' said Puffa Jacket, 'and there is another circle next to the famous one, but because it isn't called a henge, nobody bothers about it.'

He said the other circle of tree trunks is still revealed when the tide is back far enough. At its centre are two bits of wood, and he stretched out his hands to describe the span of them and they were clearly also meant to carry a corpse. He had also seen the remains of the wattle fence that had surrounded it. 'You find all sort of things out there,' he said, 'fish nets, baskets, Roman stuff.' As he spoke he kept staring out across the sand and towards the grey sea, with a kind of fondness as well as mystification.

35

Dawn and Rob are professional divers and in 2014 there was a lot of talk and publicity around them when they found a new stretch of forest from Doggerland out in the sea beyond the Norfolk fishing town of Cromer. I went to visit them in their cottage, which is near where I live and next to a very beautiful church where a good friend lies buried.

Dawn led me through the kitchen and into a low-ceilinged room. A black and white cat who carried himself with a lot of authority introduced himself. There was a large and murky fish tank containing two fish on the far wall close to a window and a number of framed photographs of magnified and brilliantly coloured sea creatures.

Dawn and Rob were both wearing jogging trousers and identical Crocs shoes, which somehow gave them a shared identity. I sat in an armchair while they sat convivially side by side on the sofa.

I never quite got around to explaining what I was doing with this book, beyond expressing an interest in Doggerland. I did mention that I had been fishing for mammoth from the Dutch coast and with surprising vehemence Rob said, 'They don't just get mammoth, you know. There's a whole lot of fish come up in their trawling nets, all of them broken and bruised and as good as dead. You can't fish for bones without catching fish.'

He said the Dutch trawling industry has been a disaster for the underwater environment, because of the use of boom nets which cause every square inch of the bed of the North Sea to be scraped bare. It's like ploughing.a field, taking all the earth away and then sieving it. There are some areas which are known to carry wrecks on them and they are left more or less alone because it is tedious to fish there, but if I am thinking of a landscape beneath the sea's surface I can forget it. It's an empty, featureless prairie. The Dutch are supposed to be good environmentalists but all fishermen are the same, they don't care about nature, they just want to smash and destroy it.

Sitting beside him, Dawn listened and said nothing. Her short pale hair was dyed into a mass of rainbow colours, rather like the soft tentacles and unlikely bodies of the marine creatures in the photographs.

I asked about the forest. They found it early in 2014 and not long after the big winter storms of December 2013 which shifted thousands of tonnes of sand beneath the ocean. Dawn was swimming from Cromer but the water was murky and somehow she got carried further out to sea than she meant to go, to an area where the water was quite clear, and there it was, close to the chalk reef that offers shelter to all sorts of creatures: a forest of trees, flattened and battered, but a forest all the same.

'It's very restful underwater,' said Dawn, like someone who was thinking aloud rather than making conversation. She trained as a microbiologist, but mostly does unpaid voluntary work; she also has a job doing analysis of what are called *colonisation plates* for the Natural History Museum. Divers all around the country are asked to fill out forms and in that way a database on marine species and seabed types is being built up and can be consulted by anyone who is interested. 'It's raw data,' she said.

I asked if they could identify the fleshy thing I had found at Holme. I described it. 'Dead man's fingers,' said Rob at once and Dawn pottered off to look for one and came back with a biscuit tin filled with lots of smelly bits of shell and seaweed, bone and wood. The tin didn't contain a dead man's finger, but she pointed out some hornwrack which looked like a scruffy bit of seaweed; she said it is a member of the Bryozoa family. It's a colonial animal and each member makes a microscopically tiny square box to live in and the boxes build up to form bigger structures rather like coral, all working in combination together, but still looking like nothing more than a bit of seaweed.

I picked up a white bivalve with a very rough shell. 'Piddock,' said Dawn and I realised that although I knew about piddocks making holes in wood and chalk, I had never known until now what a piddock looked like.

'Some people call them angel wings,' said Rob and he explained how they work like a drill bit, slowly rotating, pointed tip down, serrated shell-tooth grinding, as they burrow their way into whatever it is they want to enter.

Rob spoke about the forest. It's half a mile or so out from the shore and it's lodged among the chalk reef which hasn't been trawled for the last hundred years or more. The chalk reef is the longest in Europe, maybe in the world. The trees must have spread out across this part of Doggerland, who knows how far, but these are the last survivors, covering an area of some three to four hundred metres. They were hidden under a blanket of clay and the weight of their trunks held them down in its grip and that is why they didn't bob off and disappear. Everything is in a state of flux, the underwater tides are on the move and one year the chalk has deep crevices cutting into it and the next year it doesn't; one year a cap of clay envelops all the trees and the next year the clay has gone and the trees are exposed.

Rob switched on the huge television screen so we could watch the films he has made of the forest bed. I see a bulky object like a rolled-up blanket covered in a soupy mud and that is a tree trunk. I see a paradise of sorts, in which strange creatures congregate around the protection of the trees and the chalk reef, their luminous displays like something you might come across in a posh supermarket. There are squirts and hydroids and razor shells, all waving their frothy parasols to catch passing specks of food. There are poisonously coloured starfish and anemones and a fat thing called a sunstar which is a foot wide and feeds on its smaller starfish relatives. Most of the crabs have little waving hydroids growing like cartoon thoughts out of their heads which are also their backs. The mottled grey lobsters with their endlessly enquiring red antennae look sleek and elegant. They come out from under the protection of wood and chalk to watch Dawn in her diving suit, to find out what sort of a thing she might be. A lobster can reach the age of a hundred and a sea bass can be twenty-five years old and more than four feet in length, but few if any of these creatures are able to complete their natural lifespan and so the strength of the entire species is being weakened. Rob told me that fishermen are forbidden to catch tiny crabs but they catch them all the same and stamp on them and use them for bait. The accumulation of sad facts swirls about in my head like clouds of disturbed sediment.

Rob and Dawn can only go diving in the warmer months and when the sea is calm and clear. They usually swim out from Cromer beach and they accompany other divers, to show them the forest. Once they have got to it or to other areas that might contain bits of it, they rarely spend more than three hours underwater, making films and taking photographs and simply looking at what is there.

Dawn, sitting on the sofa, contemplated the memory of all she had seen. 'It's very restful underwater,' she said again and she looked rested, just thinking about it.

36

Tim Holt-Wilson, whose theory of process echoes so closely my own thoughts, said that we should go to Frost's Common in Norfolk. He said it was a good place to see pingo ponds that were formed during the end of the last Ice Age, and the unkempt wildness of the place might give me an idea of what Doggerland looked like.

So there we were on a warm grey day in December. We parked and entered a rather odd wood, or maybe I mean a former wood because although there were no grand oaks and chestnuts booming on about all they had witnessed over the rolling progression of the centuries, there were lots of dignified and drooping holly trees and sweet-smelling box trees and a mixture of birch and willow and pine in all the stages of their lives.

The land tilted and dipped like a choppy sea and there were no clear paths. We came to the first of the pingo ponds; it was a bright pea-green colour, more big puddle than pond, with alder trees growing straight out of the water. Their trunks looked quite spiky and flimsy but the roots that held them had turned into bulbous islands.

The whole area of Frost's Common was peppered with pingos and their colour gave them a science fiction look, as if something tentacled and terrifying might emerge and blink its red eye at any intruders. I took a few photographs but wondered if this would diminish the memory of what I was seeing.

We walked on. Still no paths, or at least the vague and inconsequential paths we occasionally followed seemed to have been made by deer or cattle. Each pingo appeared stranger than the last, and in between them there was the scrubby wood and a lot of thick moss growing on tree stumps and anywhere else it could make a cushion of itself. Tim discovered a *Fuligo septica*, a slime mould also known as dog vomit, and he said that slime moulds crawl very slowly from one perch to the next. This one was a fluorescent orange, motionless as far as I could tell and vaguely malevolent.

I saw a frog, which was odd for the time of year, and a tiny newt lying curled under a white stone that I had picked up because it looked like the bone of some vast beast. I saw a deer, slipping between the trees and disappearing even while it was still there, and I stood for a while to watch a stalk of dead bracken caught in a current of air that made its upper half twist and turn in an awkward little dance while everything around it kept still.

We emerged into an open area known as Cranberry Rough, with swampy meadows and shallow expanses of lake water and straggly clumps of alder and willow that don't mind having their red-tinged roots standing in the water. This was once the site of a large lake, and studies of the lowest level of the lake's basin found it to contain the silts and sands that had been blown across the surface of the exhausted land when it first emerged from under the ice during the end of the last Ice Age. Scientific studies of the fossil pollens held within a nine-metre-thick basin of mud chronicle the emergence of a sparse covering of pine and birch trees, and as the weather grew more mild these were replaced by thick forests of hazel and oak, alder and elm. The rich finds of worked flints from ten thousand years ago indicate that this was a very important hunting and fishing ground for the people of Doggerland.

The lake, which became known as Hockham Mere, was mentioned in the twelfth century, but it was already silting up in Tudor times and by the 1700s it had become a marsh, until the marsh was sucked dry by the spread of alder and willow. Recently the area has been cleared of most of the trees and so it is beginning to revert to its Doggerland days and some of the original birds and wildlife have returned.

It was a curiously anonymous expanse, ringed by lines of pine trees in the far distance, with some of the swamp trees still tangling around in the shallow muddy water, but in spite of its lack of feature or perhaps because of it, there was a vague sense that indeed this place had once been something else. No lake, but an awareness of the absence of a lake and containment that a lake gives.

I saw a movement in the water which could have been an eel. I glimpsed the whiteness of an egret and heard the jangling cry of geese, just two of them flying out from the trees making a huge noise within the silence. Then a flock of teal passed overhead; there were maybe a hundred of them and when they turned in unison their bodies flicked over from the blackness of a silhouette to a grey and luminous shimmer with hardly any substance to it.

In the silence that returned after the geese and the teal I became aware of the soft fizz and chatter of small birds, small sounds you only hear if you disentangle them from the modern noises of a day, the grumble of a military plane, the rumble of traffic on a road somewhere.

In the distance we could see shaggy brown cattle, the old sort from Eastern Europe which don't mind getting their feet wet in such a soggy land. We were planning to follow a causeway, walking past them and then making a sweep over to the far bank of the lake, which was where Tim had found a lot of worked flints some years ago, but at this point he realised he had not got his mobile phone. He remembered putting it into his rucksack and now the pocket of the rucksack was open and the mobile was not where it should be. It must have jumped out, escaping into the wild while the going was good.

We decided to retrace our steps. We had been walking for maybe an hour and a half, little zigzag progressions and circumnavigations of the sort that might be made by foraging animals.

The first stretch was easy with the soft mark of our own footsteps to show us where we had been, but once the ground became harder the footsteps vanished and everything looked both familiar and new. Tim asked me to phone his mobile, but no sound rang out in the wood, just a disembodied voice telling me to leave a message. We passed lots of pingos but I could not be sure if they were the same pingos I had seen before. A misty rain started to fall and a skittering breeze dislodged the last of the oak leaves and they sounded like a heavier rain. I kept pulling up the hood on my jacket and then lowering it because it was such an enveloping thing. It was a charity-shop jacket with declarations on the label about being breathable and waterproof, but it let the rain in while also making me damp from my own sweat. I noticed a holly tree bitten into the conical shape of an artificial Christmas tree by cattle and that was something I had certainly not seen before.

When we got back to the car, Tim's mobile was in the boot, oblivious to all the fuss. We drove to the other side of the lost lake, to the area where so many Mesolithic remains had been found, but the ground was covered by a tightly sealed skin of grass and roots and low vegetation and whatever lay beneath it was out of sight. Tim remembered that the Forestry Commission was digging trenches for planting pine trees when he was last here and they must have been bringing up the flints in the digging.

37

Tim said we should also have a look at what's left of the estuary where the River Yare meets the sea at Yars-mouth, later known as Great Yarmouth. Once it was part of the marsh and fertile plains that stretched out into Doggerland, and then in Roman times when the estuary was much wider, longer and deeper it than it is now, it carried big ships for many miles inland and defensive watchtowers were built along its banks from which soldiers could keep guard against the incursions of pirates and raiders.

We arranged to meet by the church in the village of Haddiscoe. I was as always early. The church appeared to be stranded on a mound of higher ground in an area of flatness and the graves in the cemetery were leaning at drunken angles as if they had only just managed to withstand the force of a great flood that had tried to overwhelm them.

The Norman porch had a worn stone carving above the door leading into the church. It showed a figure sitting on a throne with his arms raised, his hands holding what must be two torches, although to my modern eyes they resembled two ice-cream cones. The armrests of the throne had the same spindly energy as his legs and his raised arms, so that he looked like a large insect, poised there on the wall and about to leap down on whoever walked in without permission. Someone had sloshed a layer of whitewash over the solemn stone faces carved into the domed ceiling of the porch and they appeared rather startled by the indignity.

Tim arrived and before setting off we paused on a patch of green grass just outside the gate to the churchyard. Very casually he picked up the tip of a microlith, a worked flint no bigger than my fingernail. I could see the energy of the tapping on the stone which fashioned the sharp edges and the delicately pointed end, made to pierce through skin and into flesh. He said there was a time when he did a lot of running and he would catch sight of such flints almost unconsciously as he ran, stooping to collect them with hardly a pause in his step.

The first stage of our walk got us nowhere much. We started by a rather grand farm, the barns and cowsheds all empty and without function. A lopsided footpath sign directed us into a barricade of tall nettles and then on through muddy grass and under the branches of two fallen willow trees. We emerged among a patchwork of water meadows with clusters of heavy cattle in the distance and a hobby swooping like a swift overhead. A marsh harrier was mewing in the blue sky. My eyesight has become hopeless ever since I changed the prescription on my lenses and so with a sort of optimistic misguidedness I identified a seagull as a peregrine falcon and a roe deer as a hare. But I was good at concentrating on the small details on the ground under my feet, the water in the criss-crossing ditches, lichen on a post, a beetle on a stalk of grass.

The path remained vague but according to Tim's Ordnance Survey map we needed to climb over a gate and join the cattle. Once they had seen our approach they hurtled towards us, all exhaled breath and trampling feet under the bulk of their bodies, united in the fierce courage of a crowd mentality. My father used to say that if you were in a field of obstreperous bullocks or heifers you must sing hymns to them and that would calm them down: 'The Church's One Foundation' worked especially well. Neither Tim nor I were willing to try and so we prepared to turn back the way we had come, but before we left we sat for a while to gather our dignity. We were next to a ditch filled with a carpet of plants, including bog beans and something called water soldiers which I once had in a pond and the soldiers marched with such determination that they overwhelmed all the opposition. In the clear spaces between the greenness, water beetles were spinning to the surface like pinpoints of light with no body visible and crowds of glinting sticklebacks darted like bigger sparks, their sides flashing. I remembered reading that the people of Doggerland were thought to have mashed up sticklebacks and used them as a sort of oil.

We drove on a bit further and stopped at the Roman estuary fort known as Burgh Castle. Bright sunshine, a buffeting wind and the scent of new-mown hay. The castle is mostly its own outline, the remains of thick external walls so weather-beaten they could be mistaken for geological formations. Knapped flints erupt with a casual energy out of the rough but strong cement that holds them, interrupted by steady lines of red clay tiles which also looked as if they had been laid down by the accretion of time. I kept hoping to see some proof that all this really was the work of men: initials scratched on a stone, perhaps, or a rude drawing dug into the clay before the tile was fired, but there was nothing.

We walked down to the edge of the estuary. It's quite narrow these days, hemmed in and controlled by metal banks and steel nets, and the marsh has mostly been drained although there are still a few whispering reed beds and patches of glossy grasses and unexpectedly bold flowers growing in the salty mud. The high reeds made me feel as if I had ceased to exist, but Tim was tall enough to gaze out across the tops of them.

A land that was water before it became land before it became water, before it became land again. The noise of the reeds in the wind, the wind in the reeds. The wind as much alive as I am. A cormorant bobbing back to the water's surface, the fish in its beak making a struggling descent down its throat, also part of who I am within the world.

We left the estuary and went back to the higher ground close to the castle. Where the marsh had been drained and turned into meadow land I saw the brown gleam of a hare leaping from cover and racing beyond my line of sight.

A couple of weeks later, I was back in Norfolk, helping my friend Jayne who was moving into a new house with her new husband. We carried boxes upstairs and carried boxes downstairs and teetered on a stepladder while unscrewing a curtain rail and teetered again, trying to dismember a wall cupboard that resisted dismemberment. Jayne wanted to go to a local scrapyard from where she had bought an old table and so we did that.

The scrapyard was one of those chaotic compounds in which human artefacts are collected at random and left to fend for themselves in the rain and the weather. Open-doored fridges that can never again be made to work; a heap of white dinner plates filled with green water and balanced on a car fender; the laminate on a laminated table splitting into all its layers, with moss growing between them.

I picked up a slab of baked clay; it was a bit more than a foot long and maybe an inch and a half thick. It looked old and it had a nice biscuit colour. There was an odd row of marks that must have been made in the clay while it was still soft and there were other marks that appeared to have been scratched after the clay had hardened. I carried the tile over to the scrap-metal man. 'Three quid. It's not Roman, if that's what you're thinking,' he said and I paid him.

Jayne emailed a photo of the tile to her husband, Peter, who was out of the country. He replied, *My guess is it's 1,800 years old. Various things are scrawled on it, some of them very probably at much later dates. The clearest graffito is towards the bottom. The first four letters are FIAS, second person singular present subjunctive of FIO . . . meaning 'Let it/ him/ her be'. . . . The A in FIAS is written as a Greek alpha, hinting that the writer hails from an eastern province of the Roman empire . . . The next six letters appear to be SEVERO, the dative or ablative form of Severus and likely to denote the tough and unyielding soldier who became emperor near the end of the second century* AD. *He paid his soldiers well, which made him popular with them, but as a ruler he was universally hated.*

In 208 he sailed to Britain to try to pacify the north which was being ravaged by marauding Picts and he died in York in 211 . . . We can't quite see what follows but if I am right, the rest of the graffito might mean something like 'successor' or 'victor'. But why Norfolk? There were some Roman structures built in a combination of flint, mortar and brickwork around the 3rd century BC . . . *such as the Saxon shore fort of Burgh Castle.*

The clay tile is on the plan chest in my husband's studio. Now that I know the words are words I can see them at once in all their immediacy and I can see a man drawing them into the soft clay with the tip of his finger, or perhaps he is using the rounded end of a stick.

I have put the tile next to a section from the skull of a whale that I found quite recently, lodged in the lowest layer of the cliff at Covehithe. At first I had no way of guessing what it might be until a friend pointed out the thick flutings of bone that are needed to protect the cavity of the brain of a creature that dives deep into the ocean. Side by side the two objects share the same colour and something of the same rough texture, so that in spite of all their differences it looks as if they are in conversation with each other.

38

The drawings that accompany the time songs are by the Spanish painter Enrique Brinkmann. I met him when I was seventeen which means he must have been twenty-seven. We spent four weeks together although it might have been two. I spoke no Spanish and he spoke no English but perhaps it was easier to not have to explain oneself. *'Habla algo!'* he said. *'Habla algo!'* I answered like Echo in the story.

I had no doubt that my destiny was now sealed with this almost stranger and although we never again lived together we did keep in contact. Year after year I wrote him letters in my ungrammatical and what he called medieval Spanish and stumbled my way through his replies. It didn't seem to matter how little information we managed to communicate, there was always a sense of a shared understanding.

Sometimes I would send him visual images: a shell known as a Hebrew scroll, a few words written on a sheet of paper printed in Sanskrit, or on the flimsy squares of paper money that in China are given to the dead so they can pay their way in the other world. He replied in the language of his delicate drawings augmented by a few words: one on a very big sheet of tissue paper, another across a legal document already covered in the flourishes and curlicues of eighteenth-century handwriting.

When I was starting this book I wrote to tell him what I was doing and asked if he might make me a series of drawings for the songs. I said they were simple poems dealing with subjects that could otherwise be difficult or even tedious to explain: carbon dating, for instance . . . and I looked that up in my Spanish dictionary.

He said he would try. He then said he planned to spend a week in an area in northern Spain called the Coast of the Dead which he felt would be a suitable place to do the work. After a while he sent me twenty-five drawings. There were a hundred of them, but he had destroyed the others.

The drawings are as close as I could imagine to what I had imagined they might be; for me they seem to sing beside the songs, as if they are occupying a space in a parallel time.

39

I arranged to meet Martin Bell at Goldcliff on the edge of the Severn Estuary, close to the drowned island where people used to live and the vanished river that once meandered through a salt marsh and reed beds; barefoot children pausing to check the woven fish traps, to stare at the hoof marks of deer, frightening the big wading birds: the crane and spoonbill, stork and heron whose black, white and grey feathers conceal them within the watery mirage of their surroundings.

A bright warm day. No wind. Martin has an IKEA bag and a plastic toolbox. I have a little rucksack and we are both wearing wellies and waterproof trousers. We walk up concrete steps to the top of the sea wall from where we look out across the glistening expanse of the estuary at low tide. We clamber down on to scattered boulders coated in bladderwrack, careful not to slip and fall, and off we go, in search of the Mesolithic.

Martin points out the vague hump of mud and shingle to the south, which is what is left of the island. The boulders are replaced by stretches of mud and I follow carefully in the track of his footsteps. 'Good King Wenceslas's servant,' I say, but he doesn't hear me, striding ahead. He reminds me of myself, bent forward to look down at what might be there and stopping every so often to pick something up. He has been collecting fossils since childhood and at school they called him Quasimodo because of his hunched posture.

He pauses to explain things and I make notes with a pencil in a battered notebook that will soon be smeared with pale mud. 'Devil's toenail,' he says, and turns to give it to me and I am surprised again by how much these stone shells look like the shed toenails of an old and not very pleasant person. He says he has found lots of coprolites here, big ones from a fish, probably an ichthyosaurus, but he can't be sure; you can see the little bones they have swallowed if you have a good magnifier.

He says he hopes the tide will pull back far enough for us to reach the clay laminates and there with any luck we'll find a bit of charcoal from a hearth fire, a bit of worked flint, cooked bone, that sort of thing; possibly footprints as well, human, animal or bird, we'll see. Our first stop is a big lump of something covered in bright green weed as well as knobbly bladderwrack. There are other similar lumps of its kind close by, half swallowed by the mud, half struggling to clamber out of it. 'Oak trees from the very end of the Mesolithic,' says Martin, '4100 to 3880 BC. If you go deeper down you get to the earlier forest, 5800 BC. We make maps of the position of the trees and cut bits off for ring dating and sample peat for pollen and beetle studies as well. That way we learn everything we need to know about the date, the climate and the landscape.'

By now we are walking across a patch of pale and glutinous mud and I am very careful to step into the deeper imprints of his feet. There are scatterings of smaller stones where the surface is more solid and the mud that coats them looks like melted milk chocolate. There are also patches where the outgoing tide has washed the little stones clean, revealing their complex palette of umber and grey, black and white. I begin to find fossils: three ammonites, a devil's toenail and something that Martin tells me must be a coprolite, although I am not convinced.

'I haven't seen it this good for ages,' he says and we are standing in one corner of an area of some twenty by twenty metres where he and his team did a thorough three-year study, starting in 2001. They were looking for evidence of ancient woodland from the Iron Age, but also found the late Mesolithic.

We walk a bit further out towards the receding sea and now the mud is interspersed with raised patches of dove-grey clay, sometimes washed clean and sometimes lightly sprinkled with bright orange sand. We stop by a newly emerging clay ledge, built up in thin layers which I realise must be the laminates. If I want to I can turn this rippled cliff – not more than two feet high – into a huge landscape, a sort of Yosemite Park with me as a tiny person no bigger than an insect, gazing at its grandeur.

'Try not to stand on it,' says Martin and I try. He explains that this was the site of a densely populated campsite with lots of charcoal traces from campfires, worked flints, hazelnuts, fish bones, the bones of deer and aurochs, all embedded in the clay. He uses a small builder's pointing trowel to prise out a lump of charcoal for me to look at. Eager to join in, I lift out something the size of my fingernail and he says it's cooked bone, deer probably. He asks where I got it from and I look at the clay and have no idea, but I make a rough guess. He produces a satellite locating device looking rather like a mobile phone and places it next to where I think I found the bone; then he makes a note in his notebook and puts the bone in a plastic pocket and the plastic pocket goes into the toolbox.

We find a little square piece of stone which is probably from a hearth. Then a blackened hazelnut, perfect for carbon dating because they live for just one year. He prises a bit of flint from out of the clay and says it is a broken fragment from a pot-boiler: you heat flints in the fire and drop them in a wooden bowl or a skin bag filled with water and three good-sized stones will bring the water to the boil. Now that I am accustomed to looking at it, I can see that the clay is thickly flecked with these hieroglyphic stories that make me think of the drawings Enrique made when he was staying on the Coast of the Dead in Spain.

We walk further out on this wet new land that is steadily emerging. Here there is a much wider and lower expanse of clay, marked with little metal pointers and plastic tags from previous researches. Martin dips a plastic bowl into the shallow sea and washes off the scattering of sand to reveal something which he says is a human footstep. It's no longer in good condition and it looks like nothing at all, but next to it is the clear imprint of a crane's foot, a beautiful splayed leaf shape in which you can see the articulation of the toe bones and get a sense of the weight of the body of the bird pushing down. It's either an extinct species or today's common *Grus grus,* which was probably much bigger then, with more food to eat and more time to grow fat.

We see other cranes walking by in another realm, and the single hoof of a deer, and humans that I can more or less recognise from the shape and size of their feet, but what impresses me most of all is the constellation of little pockmarks imprinted on the flesh-like softness of the clay and made by the rain that was falling on one particular day between 5500 and 5200 BC. As I look I can hear the pattering sound and I can feel the wetness of it soaking into my hair and skin. The crane has flown away, the children have gone, but the rain goes on falling.

The tide is pulling further and further back; apparently the seabed is only exposed like this for a few days every month and we are lucky with the brightness of the sunshine, the washed stones, the gentle lap of the waves. We are on a patch of harder ground again and I am busy in my search for fossils, my pockets rattling with the weight of the ones I have found already. I pick up a pale piece of flint, white, but marked with streaks of grey and black as if the colours had run like ink on paper. It is an oddly shaped flint brought to a long narrow point at one end, with something like a backbone to it and very sharp edges along its

231

sides. I show it to Martin and ask him if it is interesting and he lets out a yelp as if he has stubbed his toe.

He regains his composure and says he's pretty sure that we are looking at a tanged point, otherwise known as a Font-Robert Point. It's the fourth of its kind to be found here on the estuary and one of eleven examples from the whole of the British Isles. The distinctive flint stone comes from a chalky area some forty miles to the south-east. 'The Gravettian culture,' he says. You can put the date between twenty-three thousand and thirty-two thousand years ago. They were the ones who made those heavy-breasted Venus figurines. They walked across from France during the Ice Age, using pockets of time that lasted for a thousand years or so when there were warm snaps in the weather. Not many of them, perhaps just one family group who were over here for half a dozen generations or less. They were used to wandering very widely. Exactly the same design of tanged points have been found in a burial site on the Gower Peninsula in south Wales and at other sites across Northern Europe.

He asks me to show him exactly where I had found it and this time I have a much better idea. He photographs it lying on the mud and among the pebbles. He locates it with his satellite device, he photographs me holding it and smiling. He says he will write a paper on it. He says a student of his had found one of these a few years ago but she stuffed it in her rucksack and only produced it when they were back at the café and by then she had no recollection of exactly where it had been picked up.

More than five hours have passed when we begin to make our way back towards the sea wall. The tide has already covered the land where the crane had walked and the rain had fallen and the shallow waves were pulling in on all sides but Martin is in no hurry to go and so we potter on.

We pause to look at the traces of several lines of Mesolithic fishing traps that came into view just three months ago. Such traps have been found in Denmark and Holland but never in England and Martin had been looking for them since 1991, thinking they must be here somewhere. The stubbed heads of a little wooden post protrudes a couple of inches out of the mud and then I can just distinguish the tops of little sticks which are the wattle fence leading to another post, on and on for about a hundred yards. They date from *c.* 5000 BC. It would be difficult and expensive to excavate them and even more difficult and expensive to preserve them once they were out of the water, but what matters is that they are here and a moment in time has been recorded.

Children are checking the fish traps, the crane is lifting its bedspread wings, a thin line of smoke is rising from a campfire, the rain has stopped. And there within another layer of that same picture a man is turning a white stone into a weapon that can spear a mammoth or a bison and as he works on it little chips of stone are flying off, black and white and grey like the feathers of marsh birds.

40

I had contacted Jim Leary because of his book about Doggerland in which he imagines the consequences of the rising sea levels: people trying to save their lives as the territories they had known so intimately became a flooded underworld.

We met one morning at the Royal Academy in London. We sat at a low table in the cafeteria, surrounded by the clatter of crockery, the murmur of people and curiously dim lighting, which made it feel as if night had already fallen. The American Abstract Expressionists were on show in the upstairs rooms.

We started on Doggerland, but quickly moved to the new book Jim is writing about the nature of walking. He told me of the skeleton of a Bronze Age boy found in a recent dig in Wiltshire and how tests have shown that he had the extra bone growth you see in athletes and this could only be caused by an awful lot of walking. From measuring the isotopes in the teeth you can find out where the boy was born and his bones offer clues about his health and diet, but what remains a mystery is where he was walking to or from and, above all, why he was walking so much.

Jim said that the process of walking can change your view of the world and yourself within the world. I thought of a ten-day walk I did with my husband on the Alta Via that follows the backbone of the Ligurian Alps. Much of it was originally made by Neolithic shepherds, the carefully fashioned stone paths worn smooth by their feet and by the sharp hooves of their animals. I remembered the steady quiet that surrounds you as you move between the far distance of where you have been and the far distance of where you are heading. Thoughts and worries and fears lose their urgency, dissolving within the slow rhythm of your movement. The path becomes the trajectory of a whole life, like those paintings in which you see a saint setting out on his journey from birth to death, the entire story contained within the one landscape.

Jim said that for him archaeology is an act of remembrance, even if you are remembering things you never consciously knew. The actual process of excavation is what delights him most, when he is fixing on where to start and then stripping the first turf off the topsoil in order to enter the darkness that lies beneath it. More often than not it's just soil that you find, but occasionally you come across a pristine landscape.

Between 2006 and 2008 he led an excavation of Silbury Hill in Wiltshire. It was built over a period of a hundred years four thousand years ago and was first excavated in 1849 and then again in the 1960s. It has always seemed as if the hill must contain some secret: a dead warrior, treasure, anything to put a stamp on its value and importance for the people who erected it, but the mound is nothing more than itself. It holds a kaleidoscope of different soils, gravels and big stones. It also holds a few simple discarded tools, an entire ants' nest, some perfect insects – their blue-green carapaces gleaming like jewels – seeds and berries and an area of slightly yellowed flattened grass, as if a family had been camping there on the previous night.

The mound was not especially visible from far away and it's unlikely that it retained its original chalk whiteness for long. At some stage in its construction, small boulders were put into it, 'scattered like currants in a bun', but no one knows why; maybe people imagined seeing the stones within the soil, just as the inhabitants of Doggerland must have imagined seeing the hidden gifts that lay beside the remains of their dead.

Jim said that in an attempt to understand Silbury Hill, he had been reading about the American Indians who were building similar but smaller mounds when the first Europeans arrived and recorded what they saw. Everyone would gather together to listen to the story of how the world was made by a creature who dived into the great ocean and brought up a lump of mud and this mud swelled and grew until it had become the place they now inhabited. As they listened, the people participated in the story, taking handfuls of earth and making their own mound and from this simple act of imitation, the distant past was brought into the present moment and everyone could share in its immediacy.

Our conversation was over, but before Jim left to meet a colleague he offered to take me on a walk around the Silbury Hill area and then he could tell me what lay beneath the surface of a landscape that is thick with round barrows and long barrows and complex sequences of banks and ditches, as well as the buried remains of wooden structures and the jumbled or carefully assembled bones of the dead.

And so, several months later, I took a train to a station that I used to know very well during a time in my life that now feels as distant from me as the life of a stranger. I was early and so I sat in a café in which pop music from the radio was combined with the circling repetition of world news on a big television screen and with the bird-like screeches of a little boy who sat and stared at me, keeping his back to his family and drinking a purple liquid from a plastic bottle.

Jim arrived in his car and we set off. We drove alongside Silbury Hill, which appeared suddenly and looks like nothing special until the moment you are about to pass it and you see this strange and steep-sided green blancmange in its entirety.

We reached a car park where we met Dave Field, an archaeologist who worked with Jim on Silbury Hill and other projects. A misty rain was falling, throwing a haze over our surroundings and distorting all sense of the solidity of things. We followed a wet path towards the spine of the chalk hills of Pewsey Downs, the thin ridge of the Vale of Pewsey on one side and Stonehenge out of sight in the distance beyond.

Our first stop was a dew pond; empty of water and overgrown with nettles, it looked as if a falling meteor might have made this unexpected dip in the landscape. Dew ponds have been dug and lined with clay on the porous body of the chalk ever since the first domesticated cattle were grazed here, almost six thousand years ago. Awkwardly shaped boulders were lolling around the edges of this one and these were sarsens, the same stone that was used in constructing the big uprights at Stonehenge and was hidden within Silbury Hill. The name is a shortening of Saracens and describes their apparent foreignness in such a smooth landscape. The ones around the dew pond were as big as sofas and looked like lumps of soft mud that you could mould into different shapes with your hands. These stones had metamorphosed from sand after the Cretaceous Epoch and the strange tubes and rounded holes that riddled their surfaces were made by the roots of palm trees that once grew in their long-ago soil.

When we walked to the crest of the hill we jumped into the Neolithic world; the land worked into the shape of ditches and high banks that were clearly serving a purpose although no one is quite sure what they were supposed to be keeping in or keeping out. Around six thousand years ago, the same time in which the last islands of Doggerland were vanishing and the people from there were trying to establish new lives in unknown territories, the first of the farmers were moving in with their livestock and the seeds of edible plants to be sown and cultivated and harvested. Jim thought that perhaps the vague outline of enclosures we were looking at were used in big seasonal gatherings here: crowds of people who scattered over the whole region, feasting together, trading cattle and women, weapons and tools, telling stories, singing songs.

So where were the hunter-gatherers in all of this? I had somehow presumed that there was a gradual overlap between the two peoples: the farmers needing to hunt, the hunters learning to cultivate the land and to keep livestock. While we were walking, Jim said this was probably true, but there was so little evidence to hold on to, and recently new DNA studies have been changing all the preconceptions. Now it is thought that at least 90 per cent of the hunter-gatherers disappeared without trace. For something like that to have happened means there must have been violent and dramatic confrontations, remembered in stories that have since been forgotten.

The farmers had such a different relationship with the land and the life that it supported. They were the owners and they made their mark of ownership wherever they could. They shaped the land for their purposes. They placed their dead within the land and memorialised their absent presence by erecting mounds above them. At first the bones of the dead were heaped alongside those of domesticated cattle and wild animals and no one knows what kind of rituals accompanied such depositions, but then around four thousand years ago, a greater separation seems to have been made between animals and humans and important individuals began to be entombed within their own stone chambers.

The excavations that Jim had been working on during the summer of our meeting were at a site called Cat's Brain. It had been chosen because from aerial photographs you could see evidence of what looked like a long barrow, but when the team dug down, instead of a burial they found the outline of the timber structure of a great hall, twenty-two metres long and ten metres wide, built around five thousand six hundred years ago. It seems it wasn't intended to be used as a dwelling, but as a place where a whole community could gather, as if, said Jim, the building was a metaphor of their shared existence.

We continued across the naked body of the land. Every time we passed a mound or a long barrow that had not been excavated Jim stared with an almost comical intensity at the outside skin as if he was trying to see what secrets it held. From a barrow known as Adam's Grave we looked down into the Vale of Pewsey with its patchwork of ploughed fields. Along the line where the chalk of the hills meets the fertile clay of the valley, they had found a huge midden, two hundred metres long and three metres high. It had been in use for perhaps one hundred years and they estimated it must have held the remains of a quarter of a million sheep as well as a hundred and twenty thousand cows and a thousand people.

We walked on, making a loop back towards the parking place. Soft rain was still falling. Apart from an old couple walking side by side with their Jack Russell on a lead, we had not passed anyone on the hills, nor had we seen any sign of life in the wide expanse of cultivated land in the valleys. Everything was bereft of the presence of human beings and even the sheep and cattle had been replaced by the silent cultivation of corn and wheat.

Time Song 15

I am walking with Bryony along a path
that runs above a narrow wooden road
that crosses a marsh
from one island to another.
This is what is left of Sweet Track,
the name derived not from the recollection of sweetness
but from Mr Sweet, who first discovered it.
The reeds enclose us,
the sky watches us,
the rest of the world is far away.

Bryony and her husband started work here in 1970,
digging down every fifty metres to uncover
a straight line of planks and pegs and poles,
over a mile long;
the wood blackened and broken by the passing
of close on six thousand years.

It is estimated that
twenty to thirty people built the track
within twelve months.
It is hard to tell if they were following the line of an earlier one;
it is also hard to tell if the track was constructed

For symbolic purposes:
for stepping across the still waters,
mists rising, reeds whispering,
the sudden shock of the cries of birds.
It could just as well be a simple means
of going hunting,
or a connecting link with neighbours
on the other island.

Curved pins made from yew tree wood
were casually dropped along the way;
perhaps they held long hair into a clump,
kept a cloak in place,
closed a pouch made of skin,
or nettle fibre.

Polished stone axeheads were found,
beautiful in their simplicity,
one from green-tinged jadeite
came from the Dolomite region
in northern Italy
and took at least two hundred years
to travel from south to north.
There is no way of knowing if such treasures
were accidentally dropped and lost,
or placed in the waters
to placate a discontented spirit,
or to give thanks to one who was more benign.

I am walking with Bryony,
the reeds enclose us,
the sky watches us,
the rest of the world is far away.
'You find something,' she says,
'And then you try to understand
what it is you have found.
Your thoughts are captured,
as much by a hazelnut chewed by a water vole
and how it came to rest here,
as by the jadeite axe
whose journey is just as mysterious.'

She describes the little heaps of white quartz grit
scattered at intervals along the track
and how they puzzled over them:
was it magic or medicine,
or the fashioning of some thing, since gone?

Finally they decided
it could be from the gizzards of swans
whose dead bodies lay trapped
by the wood of the track
until everything of them had vanished
apart from these glittering fragments,
bearing witness to what once had been.

Based on a walk with Bryony Coles on 22 September 2017. In a later email she wrote, 'The Sweet Track was built across a reedy swamp with a few birch and willow trees, which was followed by fen woodland and then raised bog. When people came to cut the peat in the Middle Ages, it was the uppermost peat they took, the raised bog peat, and as far as we know they were quite unaware of the different sorts of peat below and of the buried trackway.'

41

Of all the images of time passing and yet not passing, of the dead being absent and yet present, nothing for me is as vivid as Tollund Man who was found in 1950 in the bog in which he had lain for two thousand four hundred years and who still looks as if he is drifting in a quiet sleep from which he might stir and wake at any moment. I first saw photographs of him in a book called *The Bog People,* written in Denmark by the wonderfully named P. V. Glob and published in Britain in 1969 and he has been with me ever since, as familiar as anyone else whose face I hold in my memory.

This spring I got a commission to make a radio programme with my friend Tim Dee and so there we were in Jutland, walking through an area called Bjaeldskovdal where Tollund Man was accidentally uncovered by peat cutters who thought at first that he must be the branch of a tree. The peat cutters have all gone now, along with most of the peat, and the area has reverted to a sort of Doggerland landscape with wide expanses of shallow water and higher areas where salix and dogwood, heather and bilberry bushes grow, along with lots of silver birch, the silver turned a soft and dusty green. We saw some exposed patches of peat telling of what once was and pale dried clumps of sphagnum moss tumbled about on the ground, as light as sponge from a seabed.

A bog is like a riddle: neither water nor land and yet both land and water. Ten thousand years ago when the ice had retreated and the weather in north-western Europe was cold but not too cold, bogs took hold of great tracts of the sodden landscape and many bogs like this one must have been formed in Doggerland when the climate was right for such a process. They became home to a profusion of life, but they were fickle and dangerous places. A blanket bog can climb a mountain slope and break its banks and engulf a whole area and all bogs have a quicksand quality enabling them to pull anything down into their soft dark hearts, but it's only the raised bogs that have the special ability to grant physical immortality to their victims, keeping what they swallow in a hardly altered state for hundreds or even thousands of years, whether it is a leaf or a man. Bogs are also the home of sudden mists and miasmas and those self-igniting balls of fire as small as a candle flame, as big as a man's head, darting about with restless energy or glimmering and hovering enticingly over one particular spot.

Sphagnum moss in all its varieties is the plant out of which a raised bog is formed; such mosses first emerged three hundred million years ago. An ordinary peat bog can begin to take shape when dead plant litter accumulates in the still waters of a shallow lake or a marsh and as this debris builds up it is compressed into fibrous matter by its own waterlogged weight. If it becomes sufficiently poor in nutrients and oxygen, then sphagnum moss can establish itself. The moss sucks up twenty times its own weight in water that becomes as acidic as pickling vinegar. Every winter the uppermost layer dies, releasing a natural sugar compound that helps to destroy any bacteria and so the spongy structure of the dead layer is preserved and year by year the bog grows steadily higher until the living layer is separated from the water table and relies only on rain. A raised bog can reach a height of several metres and cover an expanse of several kilometres. It creates a landscape of domed cushions whose colours vary from luminous green to blood red. In the patches where the moss is absent, rounded pools of deep water are formed, so darkly stained by the peat they can appear almost black.

The sphagnum makes the surrounding water table too acidic for trees to grow, but sedges and shrubs gather close and cotton grass and heather spread out over some of its surfaces. Bog beans live in the deeper pools and sundews on the moss itself, trapping insects with their sticky jaws, while underwater bladderworts suck up tiny organisms.

In winter or in early spring when the weather is cold and the temperature of the water is not above 4 degrees C, raised bogs can preserve whatever enters their domain, whether it is the autumn leaf or the fully clothed human body, a woven basket, a pair of shoes, a dog, a wooden roadway, a canoe, a carved god, or a clay pot still holding the burnt remains of the food that was cooked in it. But in the moment when something is lifted out of the bog and into the air it begins to change and disintegrate and if it is kept in its sodden state it quickly rots.

Raised bogs have a life of their own. They twist and turn as they grow in size and this slow movement changes the position of whatever they are holding: a wooden shaft is snapped in two, the limbs of a person or an animal are shifted into unnatural positions and the head turns as if its owner has decided to stare in another direction. And because every bog has its own particular chemical composition, each one immortalises its treasures in a different way. Some might strip a body of all the calcium in the bones which then turn soft and without structure, while the keratin in skin and fingernails becomes peat-dark and as hard as old leather and every hair is kept intact but dyed a bright orange. Others destroy clothing and leather belts and hats and all trace of flesh, while leaving a perfect and intact skeleton.

The people who lived close to raised bogs harvested the dried peat for fuel and as if in return for what they had taken they placed gifts into the still pools that reflected the face of the moon or their own faces so clearly, or into the deep cuts they had made into the body of the peat. The more a bog was used, the more gifts were given, presumably to appease whatever gods and spirits lived there in the form of mists and miasmas, sudden inexplicable noises and wandering flames.

Around two thousand years ago when a rough sort of iron was first being taken from the bogs and used to make weapons and tools, then valuable but inanimate gifts were augmented with the gift of human beings. These could be the bodies of the dead defeated in a battle, but there were also human sacrifices in late winter or early spring when everything was at its lowest ebb and people must have been hungry and afraid. The life of one person, such as Tollund Man, would be offered in exchange for the life of a whole community.

Tim and I were following a path that skirted a lake scattered with little islands that looked like the pieces of a jigsaw puzzle that could easily be joined together again. The silence was broken by the occasional noisy goose and a swan or two, but the dimension of bird cry and song was mostly missing, probably because the season was too young and the first of the migrating birds had not yet arrived. The path meandered along until we reached our destination: a tall tree trunk, stripped of its bark, had been fixed in the ground like a post. It had a simple brass plaque attached to it on which was inscribed a date and the name 'Tollund Man' and the names of the two people who found him.

We sat next to the trunk on pale grasses that must have been recently covered by snow and Tim recorded the wind that was blowing through the silver birch trees to use as a background noise in the radio programme. Then he recorded us talking about where we were and why we had come here and I explained what I knew of Tollund Man's story.

After a while, damp and a bit cold, we got to our feet and continued on the path which led us to a wooden walkway built across the remains of the old bog. The brightly luminous colours of the sphagnum moss were interrupted by dark pools, and the mixture of wet land and solid water seemed as alive as a breathing thing, made dangerous by the knowledge that if you fell there were no firm edges to hold on to and if you were foolish enough to try to cross the bog's surface it might simply suck you down.

I thought of the people following the narrow wooden tracks they had made when the bog was deeper and the landscape so much wider, stretching out for miles in all directions. I thought of them navigating their canoes, or stepping precariously from one hummock of safe ground to another.

I wondered if some of them were still held within the black peat; smiling faces close by or even under our feet, and I felt dizzy with the idea of them being as uncorrupted as the dead are supposed to be when they are woken at the Last Judgment.

Tim is a bird man. On our way back I asked him rather absentmindedly what bird he would like to be if he were a bird. 'Redstart,' he said, without a moment's hesitation, probably because he had just seen one flitting among the birch trees.

Time Song 16

The weight and the power
of the bog that held him
tight in its dark embrace,
took away his youth
and replaced it with the face
of old age.

He is photographed
as he emerges into the air,
the skin creased,
the slack mouth shut,
the half-closed eyes
seeming to take in
the strangeness of the world
he has returned to.

The body has lost much of its true shape,
but the feet look as though they could stand firm
and one perfect hand is held for ever
in a gesture of benediction:
the first three fingers
folded softly
towards the palm,

the index finger slightly raised,
while the side of the thumb
rests against it,
hardly touching.

He died in winter,
made to kneel while his throat was slit
then carried naked across the bog
to a water-filled peat cutting
where he was lain face down,
lumps of peat on top of him
to keep him under.

His last meal
was a bowl of gruel,
famine food that told its story
in gossamer-thin scraps of leaf,
in tough stalk and broken twig,
seed casing and pod,
wisp of grass,
moss, two kinds of.

Traces of sixty-five plant species
turned hard and leathery by peat-juices,
were found in his stomach and intestine,
among them:
spelt and rye,
naked barley and hulled barley,

cultivated oat and wild oat,
rye grass, tufted hair grass,
wood bluegrass and lopgrass;
a capsule of gold of pleasure,
a seed of shepherd's purse,
field pennycress, thyme-speedwell,
pale persicaria and redshank.

Sheep's sorrel, curled dock, black bindweed,
hemp nettle and corn spurrey,
common mouse-ear chickweed,
wallflower and tormentil,
fat hen, goosefoot and forget-me-not
— not ever, no matter what —

Self heal, hawk's beard and pansy,
violet and long-headed poppy,
ribwort plantain and black nightshade,
— also known as deadly —
cockspur and Yorkshire fog,
clustered bellflower and spiny sow thistle.

Also sand and small stones
from the threshing floor,
eggs of the whip-worm parasite,
tiny traces of cooked meat
and ergot,
a fungal disease in cereals,

especially rye,
causing hallucination in mild cases,
coma leading to death *in extremis.*
Remember all those men, women and children,
dancing across Europe in the thirteenth century,
mad as the wind and hoping for salvation?
St Anthony's Fire they called it —
that was ergot.

But on a cold day
two thousand three hundred years ago
there was not enough ergot in Grauballe Man
to protect him from the shock of the death
that had been chosen for him.

Based on *Grauballe Man: Portrait of a Bog Body* by Pauline Asingh, Moesgård Museum/Gyldendal, 2009. Grauballe Man was discovered in April 1952, near the village of that name. He was thirty-four years old when he died in 290 BC. I went to see him in the Moesgård Museum in Jutland. He is its most famous exhibit and he lies in the heart of the building. You enter a dimly lit space and walk across a brown floor with a spongy quality that is meant to imitate the surface of a peat bog. You reach an area fenced off by plate glass, from where you can look down at the body lying in a soft brown sepulchre. You go to the floor below to gaze at him more closely but I was so shocked by what I saw, I left almost at once. During two years of careful work the original face was cosmetically stretched and lifted and as a result the battered but calm person who was there has been replaced by a strange and frightening creature, more Hollywood ghoul than human being.

42

In Danish the word for book is *bog*.

This is the story. On Saturday 6 May 1950 and not far from the village of Tollund – the name means a grove belonging to the Norse god Thor – a woman called Grete, her husband Viggo, their three children and Emil her husband's brother travelled along a sunken road in a cart pulled by two horses called Red and Grey. When they reached a small raised bog which belonged to the family, the men began cutting peat with their spades while Grete and the children laid the peats out to dry on the drying ground.

A couple of days earlier they had come across what looked like a short-handled wooden sword and now Emil's spade again hit a hard object which he thought must be a tree stump. Grete came to see. She clambered down to join the men in the cutting that was some two metres deep. She put her hand into the peat and realised later her finger must have moved between the forehead and the skullcap that Tollund Man was wearing. She scraped back the peat and uncovered the surface of the leather cap made out of eight pieces of sheepskin, fur-side inside to keep the head warm. The others helped her and they reached the face.

The man they saw was small, dark-skinned and perfectly preserved. He appeared to be lost in sleep, his eyes closed so softly you might expect to see the eyelids flickering from the workings of a dream, and, just like a dreamer, his lips were set in a private smile. He looked as though he might wake up at any moment, yawn and stretch his limbs and wonder what strange place he was in and how long he had been there.

The family had not previously found any bog bodies, not even those of animals, but they knew of the recent disappearance of a schoolboy who never came back from a bicycle trip. Perhaps this was the boy or even someone else who had been recently murdered. They hid what they had found with peat and went on with their work. They worked on the next day as well, cutting around the block in which the body lay. On Monday they went to a public telephone and contacted the police station.

A detective who also helped at the local museum in the town of Silkeborg arrived at the site, along with the museum librarian and the archaeologist Professor P. V. Glob who knew all about bogs and the bodies they could hold.

They could see the outline of the man within the block of peat. He was lying on his right side, his head turned to the west. Although some parts of the body seemed quite firm, other areas were wet and crumbly and so it was decided not to try to remove him. A carpenter was sent for and asked to bring planks to make a crate big enough to hold both Tollund Man and his bed. The news of the find had travelled and a cluster of people turned up to stare. A local newspaper reported that the body was wrapped in a fur coat, but this was only the soft, pale and fibrous layer of a type of peat called dog's flesh on which he lay.

Ten men helped to heave the crate and its heavy load out of the bog and to manoeuvre it on to the cart to which Red and Grey were harnessed. A policemen strained his heart while doing the lifting and died shortly afterwards. 'A life for a life,' said Professor Glob later when he wrote about the occasion; he had a natural gift for the dramatic. The crate travelled by cart and then by train to the National Museum of Copenhagen and for some reason the journey took eight days.

On examining him the museum specialists found that Tollund Man was naked with no sign of having worn clothes that had later disintegrated. His cap had two leather straps that went under his chin and were tied in a bow at his right temple. There was a leather belt around his waist and a long plaited leather cord tight around his neck, its length bunched up beside his left shoulder and falling down his right side. He must have been hung from a tree, just as the one-eyed god Odin was hung on the ash tree called Yggdrasil.

He was lying on a sandy layer in which no plant remains were visible and this meant that he had been put in an existing cutting far out in the bog. His body had been very carefully arranged, the limbs drawn up, the head turned, perhaps someone closed his eyes for him. He had been there for at least two thousand years.

His death had taken place during the winter when the water in the bog was cold and best suited for the mysterious process of preservation. His last meal had been a winter gruel and traces of sphagnum moss seemed to indicate that the mixture had been cooked in bog water; perhaps he had also been given bog water to drink.

The hair on his head was cut very short and there was stubble on his chin and cheeks and above his upper lip. Although his face was perfect, much of the rest of him was badly damaged, although his feet and one thumb were still intact.

There was no tradition of preserving such a macabre but human creature and no certainty as to how the job should best be done. The Copenhagen Museum wrote to the Silkeborg Museum and suggested that they should try to keep the head, the cap, the belt and the cord, while putting the rest of the body in storage, even though it would inevitably shrink and become distorted. This was agreed and the preserving process began and continued over the next two years. The head was first placed in antibacterial fluid and then in alcohol and then in something called toluol and when it finally emerged it was a bit smaller than it had been, but otherwise perfect. The Copenhagen Museum sent a bill to the Silkeborg Museum covering the cost of the chemicals and of the saucepan in which they put the head when it was ready to be returned to Jutland. There was a little ceremony to mark the event and the director of the Copenhagen Museum was photographed holding Tollund Man's head rather tentatively in both hands. It looks like a bronze sculpture rather than the remains of a human being.

I was sitting with Tollund Man in a room in the museum. I had drawn a wooden stool up close to the glass case where he lay. There were pale wooden tiles on the floor and they silenced any noise the stool might make when I moved it, and muffled the sound of footsteps. There were no windows but the walls were painted in a yellow ochre wash that made it look as if sunlight was shifting across them. There was nothing else in the room apart from a little notice by the entrance. It was like being in a church but without any god watching over me.

Tollund Man's body looked empty and wasted as if he had been left to hang in the wind on a gibbet. He lay as he was found, curled over on his side, the limbs black and shrunken, although there was an energy in the twist of his hip. His arms made me think of bat wings, his hands the wings of smaller bats.

I moved the stool to sit facing his face. He must have looked very like this when the people who were with him were closing his eyes before they covered him over. I knew it would be powerful to see him,

259

but I was not prepared for the impact of the meeting. It was as if he was about to laugh at the joke that had appeared in his dream and there was a sense that although his eyes were closed they were not fully closed and he could see me, see any one of his visitors, at the point where the eyelids let in a narrow strip of light.

When my husband was growing increasingly fragile, he often reminded me of Tollund Man and I could see the resemblance now. They had the same pattern of lines across the forehead, the same arch of the nose, the same inward smile. But as soon as my husband had died the person he had been was no longer there, while Tollund Man appeared to be still inhabited by himself.

A woman came in with her young child and they pulled up two stools and sat close to me. The mother was talking quietly to the child, but I could not understand what she was saying.

I had made an appointment with the museum director and when he arrived Tim and I interviewed him in Tollund Man's room, all three of us sitting around the glass case and its contents, a fourth person who was there with us listening to what was being said.

The museum director had a long, thin, elegant face, the skin stretched over the careful structure of the bones. He seemed both contained and content. He said he had wanted to become an archaeologist as a child when he picked up a Bronze Age potsherd and all of a sudden he had an insight into the people who made it and the time in which they lived and it was as if they stepped through and briefly entered the present moment. He said that seeing Tollund Man every day made him realise that death is not so bad; it is nothing to be afraid of.

43

A tall piece of furniture stands against a wall in this room where I am working. It's called Amberg's Cabinet Letter File and it was manufactured in the United States in the 1940s. I once saw its twin playing a bit part in an old black-and-white detective movie and felt quite proud seeing it there.

The cabinet is supposed to have thirty drawers, each one big enough for a ream of paper, but mine has always had one drawer missing which seems appropriate because it was given to me on my twenty-ninth birthday.

I use the file to organise many aspects of my life that might otherwise get lost or forgotten about. I have a drawer for fairy lights and one for photographic negatives. Old postcards have their own drawer and so do invoices and certificates, tins of shoe polish, electric plugs and book reviews. A slow accumulation of newspaper cuttings has grown so big it occupies two drawers.

Here's an interview with Iris Murdoch teetering on the edge of dementia and just beneath it a photograph of the synapses of a mouse waving at each other as they try to make the connections necessary for a mouse memory to function. Then comes a story about phantoms in the sky and how on a summer day in 1797 the image of the coast of France appeared floating above the town of Hastings, with fishing boats pulled up on to a stretch of sandy beach in Picardy. It was something to do with cold air being trapped under hot air and acting like a glass prism that bends the light to reveal far-away places hidden by the curve of the world.

The discovery of a clam shell etched with little zigzag patterns between 430,000 and 540,00 years ago is followed by the mummified bodies found in the deserts of Peru dressed in clothes of embroidered silk and human skulls used as drinking vessels and a medical explanation for Erik the Red's fiery temper. I also have an account of the excavations in Gorham's Cave on Gibraltar that took place in June 1991 and the article includes a photograph of the cathedral-like interior of the cave which was said to be inhabited by human beings for ninety thousand years or more. A team of palaeontologists was busy excavating the accumulation of sand and broken stalactites, bat guano and human traces, held in the deep layers of time. One of those involved in the work was Nick Ashton whom I met not long ago at the British Museum depot.

When I first read about the cave I thought how much I would like to visit it and now I have been there and come back.

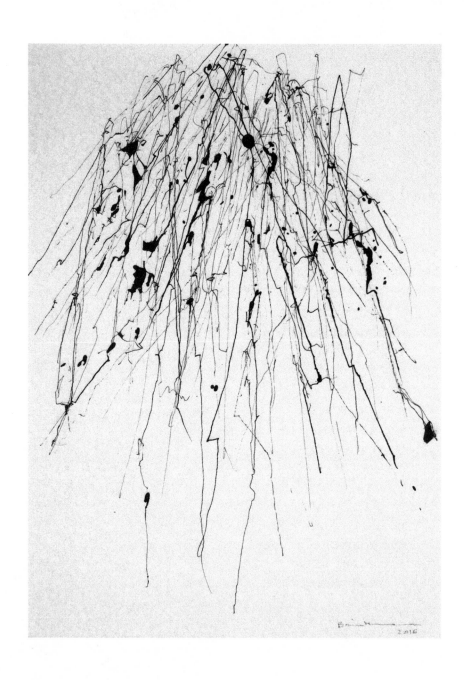

Time Song 17

The plane settles its bulk on tarmac and concrete,
here where Spain and Gibraltar meet
in a dense spread of roads and road signs,
offices and hotels, shops and petrol stations
built upon an isthmus of sand and marsh and lake.

To the east of the isthmus:
a sheer curtain drop of limestone rock,
pushed into precipitous place
by the slow collision of the tectonic plate of Africa
with that of Europe.

This rock that emerges so abruptly from the sea
once faced a landscape of sand dunes scattered with umbrella pine,
wild olive and juniper on the more solid ground
and all the spicy-scented plants of the Mediterranean.

Great flocks of wading birds working the shallow lakes,
dancing clouds of swift, swallow and martin,
the floating presences of osprey, eagle and vulture:
one hundred and forty-five avian species
found in fossil records.

The climate here was mild
even during the ages of ice,
no woolly mammoth, steppe bison
or other northern beasts,
but ibex and red deer,
lynx and leopard and scavenging hyena,
tortoise and lizard,
rabbits among the dunes.

Beyond the land's last edge:
the deep strait where one sea meets another,
and through that strait the great fish and marine mammals
followed the path of their migrations:
monk seal and beluga whale, dolphin, porpoise and tuna;
records show that here in the seventeenth century
three thousand tuna were caught on a single day.

How has it happened, the modern world?
And how will it end, when the end comes?
Abdul at the reception desk of the cheap hotel
where a cockroach appears as if by magic
every morning in the bathtub of my room
says, 'We need all this,'
waving an elegant hand towards
the forests of brick and glass,
the dark tarmac plains,
the jostling rivers of people,
the stinking herds of cars and trucks.

But then he smiles at the revelation of his own joke and says,
'At least, they say we do.'

That night, after the drunks had fallen silent,
I heard a Scops owl calling its two-note cry
as it flew above this town of fumes and chips and history,
and today I saw the perfect silhouette of a tuna
leaping out of the silver sea
close to the mouth of a cave
where human beings had their human home
for tens of thousands of years,
leaving hardly a trace of their passing.

44

There is a long descent of concrete steps that take you down a precipitous cliff on the east coast of Gibraltar. The steps follow the cliff as it makes a sharp turn to the right and then you can see a little bay of boulders lapped by the water's edge and the arched entrance to a cave that was occupied by human beings for a hundred and twenty thousand years, maybe more because any earlier evidence was washed out during a shift in the world's climate.

I was with Clive Finlayson, the director of the Gibraltar Museum. He had driven us away from the tax-evading, Queen-saluting, rubbish-dumping but wonderfully mixed-race confusion of the town and we were following a road cut into the limestone mass against which the town presses its growing weight and size. We stopped at a metal fence where a uniformed soldier greeted Clive through the barrier of wire, before he unlocked a gate and let us in. We were now on Ministry of Defence property. I was given a form to sign, which was something to do with safety rather than secrecy, and we both put on hard hats in case rocks fell on our heads.

We walked through a short tunnel, one of many tunnels that have been hacked and dynamited through the body of this rock that was once thought to mark the world's edge. This particular tunnel was called Arow Street because Mr A. R. O. Williams planned its direction and organised its execution. It emerged on to an open-air platform from where the Williams Way tunnel took up the journey. A flat-fronted concrete building with closed screens covering its windows had been pressed into an angle of the rock face. It was meant to serve as a convalescent hospital during the last war but it never progressed beyond the first stage of construction. From the platform you could see the metal handrail that belonged to the steps and, beyond that, the sunlit Mediterranean.

Down, down, down and we paused to watch a pair of ravens flying quite close and talking to each other, the harsh wide-throated sound of their conversation going back and forth between them. The Neanderthals would have heard the same birds, seen their black shapes cut into the sky and their awkward lurching movements on the land. Fossil remains from Gorham's Cave and Vanguard Cave that lies next to it have shown the cuts of stone knives on the wing bones of ravens and other birds of prey, but no marks on the breast or back and no evidence of these birds being cooked and eaten. From this it would seem that the wing feathers were collected and used as some sort of decoration.

At the base of the cliff we scrambled over what had been a concrete path until it was broken up and swept away by the force of the sea, and then we were at the mouth of the cave. Most of it is white limestone but the limestone has merged with sandstone strata which sometimes erupt into ledges that look like wax dripped from a candle. These ledges mark the shoreline of interglacial beaches that were pushed upwards in five stages in a process called *tectonics*; the higher the ledge, the earlier its formation. Remains of the uppermost ledges are close to Gibraltar's summit and were probably formed during the Pleistocene Age five million years ago. By now crag martins were swooping out of the cave, so close they almost brushed against me.

Clive was born in Gibraltar. He originally came to the cave to catch and ring the birds that sheltered and nested here and to study the heaps of their bones littering the cave floor. After a while he shifted to the

Neanderthals who had lived alongside the birds and the colonies of bats, lizards and tortoises, while the hyenas and other predators were kept at a distance by the burning of hearth fires. The Neanderthals were here for at least one hundred thousand years and then after a period of cold and drought they were gone and the cave was empty of human life for six to eight thousand years until *Homo sapiens* arrived. The new humans congregated in larger groups, but apart from that they followed the same way of life, ate the same sort of food and lit their fires and threw away their rubbish in the same places that the Neanderthals had used.

Until the rising sea levels that also flooded Doggerland, the caves looked out across a wide expanse of territory spreading out some five kilometres towards the Strait. There were many more caves along the cliff face and within the pinnacles of quartzite rock that dotted the landscape. When a palaeontologist friend of Clive's first came here, he let out a shout of revelation and said, 'My God, it was a Neanderthal city!'

This was Africa on the edge of Europe, with a microclimate that was rarely affected by the shifts of temperature a bit further to the north. The sand dunes were held firm by pine trees and other Mediterranean vegetation and even when rain was scarce, freshwater springs fed into a pattern of rivulets and lagoons. If you go diving you can still see the movement of this water as it seeps up from the seabed. Inside the largest of the caves the temperature was hardly affected by the seasons. They were warm and dry and safe places in which to be as the Ice Ages came and went.

We were in the cave now, under the shelter of an overhanging roof some thirty metres above our heads. On the left was a solid chute of rock, like a waterfall trapped into stillness. A few tatty clumps of greenery were clinging to it but Clive said that this spring, after several dry months followed by heavy rainfall, the whole rock erupted into a firework display of bright flowers that went on emerging and unfolding for a couple of weeks or more. He had never before seen anything like it.

At the front of the cave there was a wave of dark yellow sandstone and embedded within it I could see what was left of a hearth: black flecks of charcoal from the fire, the shells of limpets broken with a stone to get to the gristly meat of them, fragments of the butchered and cooked bones of ibex, nuts from the umbrella pine and a black flint tool that had been partially completed and then abandoned and left lying there until it was trapped by the sand turned into stone.

A long swathe of loose sand mixed up with broken stalactites, bat guano and everything left behind by the Neanderthals and those who followed on from them erupts from the cave's mouth like a great tongue and the deeper you dig into it, the further back in time you go. For the most recent excavations a strip of some sort of black rubber has been fixed in place with lengths of wood, so that it enters the cave like a long stair carpet that slowly ascends towards the far end.

By now the crag martins were growing accustomed to us and they began to settle in a line along a high ridge of sandstone that used to be lapped by the sea. They watched us with the friendly curiosity of their breed.

We walked up the black slope of steps which went alongside a huge and fortress-like tower of limestone, its flat top surmounted by a tall stalagmite, but I was so busy with the small details of things that I hardly noticed their presence. We reached a wooden platform and from here the cave floor had been excavated into steps, some of them marked with lines and flags or protected with some sort of covering.

The back wall of the cave was one hundred and twenty metres from the entrance, but the low autumn sunlight shone right in, illuminating everything with a yellow glow. Clive pointed to an area where a second fire used to be lit, the smoke spiralling up into the cracks and fissures in the high ceiling. This fire would have kept predators away and to the left of it there was a low arch which led to a chamber where the people had slept. Within that chamber a Neanderthal had scratched an image on the wall, a little hieroglyph of crossed lines which is currently the earliest evidence of the making of something just for the look of it. Later, *Homo sapiens* scratched drawings of the heads of horses on the same wall and made imprints of their hands.

We turned to go back and Clive told me to go ahead on my own. I climbed the three or four wooden steps and stood on the platform. It was the same sort of shock I had experienced in the rock tunnel beneath Jerusalem where Jesus made the miracle of giving sight to the blind man. The sea was molten silver and the brightness of the sun poured in through the cave's huge mouth and highlighted the silhouette of the squat tower of rock and the stalagmite that stood upon it, tall and powerful and shaped like an erect penis: the guardian or the god of the cave, triumphant and powerful and keeping watch on everything that happened, everyone who came and went.

The yellow autumn sunlight played upon the surfaces of the limestone. White and yellow in all its permutations, with the occasional tracery of bright green where water had seeped in and little mosses had grown. The stone was criss-crossed with striation marks as if it was being stretched and pulled by the process of its own birth. It was pockmarked with patterings and whorls, scoops and cracks that appeared to be breathing with life, talking to me in a whispered language I could not understand.

Clive joined me. 'Stay as long as you like,' he said. 'It is something you will never forget. The sun is in a perfect position today. Sometimes the cave's mouth frames the image of the full moon and the light of it spills in and it is quite extraordinary. I am shocked again, whenever I see it.'

He said that here, close to the fortress and its guarding figure, the people who came as visitors after the cave's inhabitants had gone brought offerings. Phoenicians came here in their boats around 800 BC and left lamps and rings, bracelets and bowls, amulets and scarabs, and later the Carthaginians gave their gifts, and these pilgrimages to the god who watched over the cave that stood at the edge of the world went on into the medieval period, but not beyond.

We walked the short distance across the stony beach to Vanguard Cave. It was smaller and less dramatic but still beautiful and for people like Clive it was very important because it had not been much visited over the years and had not been excavated and so it contained more perfect relics of the Neanderthal period. Only this July they had found the canine milk tooth of a Neanderthal and it had been taken away for analysis by someone who specialised in Neanderthal canine teeth. The cave floor was divided into sections and carefully marked where it had been excavated into sealed layers of past time. They had found evidence of several hearths and were hoping to find human footprints in an area that had once been soft mud. We looked at all this from a distance. If we were to go closer we would need to be wearing protective clothing, so as not to contaminate the DNA of the Neanderthals with our own.

Close to the mouth of Vanguard Cave, Clive showed me the remains of another sand dune turned into stone. A group of two or three Neanderthals lit a small fire. They threw a handful of mussels into the flames and you can see the shells that split and shattered. They retouched their stone tools to make them sharper, and the shards were found close to the fire and could be pieced together. They were sitting behind the shelter of the dune which meant they would be in the shade; so maybe they were having their meal in winter with a wind blowing in from the sea, or maybe it was night. They were not here for longer than twenty-four hours and then they were gone.

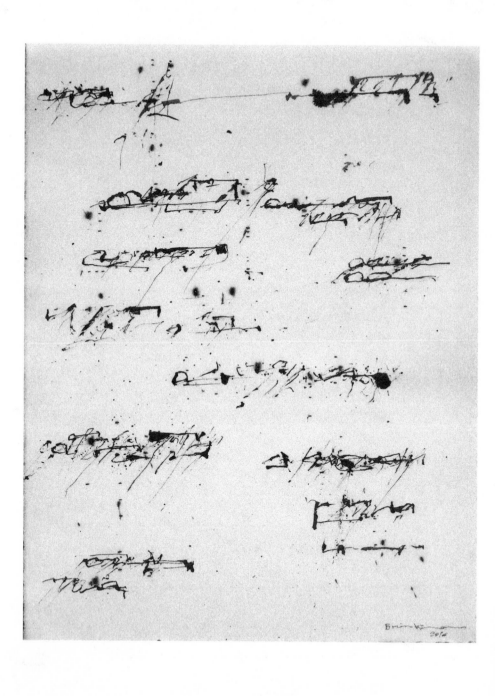

Time Song 18

Today is the anniversary
of your death,
and if today
I were to write you a letter
that you could read,
even though you are dead and read nothing,
I would say I have been looking for you
and I have not found you
but I have found traces of your absence
alongside the other absences
that rear up before my eyes like startled horses,
a wave breaking on the shore,
the moon shifting into view from behind dark clouds.

I would say I have been comforted
by the crowdedness of it all
and I would say to you who does not listen
that time is both longer and shorter
than I ever imagined:
land becomes sea, sea becomes land,
ice into desert, desert into salt marsh,
salt marsh into birds and fish, animals and people,
everything forgotten and remembered and forgotten again;

bone and stone,
footprint and tree trunk,
beetle wing and speck of pollen,
they rear up before my eyes like startled horses,
a wave breaking on the shore,
the moon shifting into view from behind dark clouds.

Then I would say to you
who does not care
one way or another:
I think it's all right,
the world will continue
even if we have gone
and that is surely something
to smile about.

45

12 February 2018 and Jayne and I have decided to watch the dusk and the dawn as they play out across the North Sea that covers whatever is left of a country called Doggerland.

We begin at the village of Cley which is on a stretch of coast near where she lives. It's not yet 4 p.m. but the sun is already going down and the luminous turquoise of the sky is streaked with red and apricot, buttery yellow and candyfloss pink.

We walk along a path that goes through the reeds but runs parallel to the road and so we are accompanied by the strange animal growl of cars. We pass a notice explaining that these freshwater marshes are fed from springs bubbling up through the Late Cretaceous chalk beds. I suppose it must be the same process that created the pingos I saw with Tim. I watch my own long shadow moving beside me. During a brief lull of cars I can hear sparrows being noisy in a bush and a chicken celebrating the laying of an egg.

The path turns sharp right and becomes a raised track that crosses reed beds and swampy meadows and spreading expanses of water. Lots of birds. I recognise oystercatchers and something which must be a whimbrel, a few egrets, pochards with their wonderful chestnut-brown heads and a heron. A man heading back to the village is shouting into his mobile. He says, 'Would it be helpful if we got hold of some recent analysis not sent by the original company?' I write his words in my notebook. His two children and a black dog follow silently in his wake.

My eye is caught by a moving flurry of white feathers on the bank that leads down from the track. It's the body of a tern brought to life by the wind; its head is raised in a sort of defiance and its beak is bright red and very sharp.

We reach the shore. Razor shells, oyster shells, whelks, a crab claw. I pick up a pale flint that contains a little picture: a black shape like the silhouette of the head and shoulders of a man and next to the head is a rounded black bubble that could be his thoughts. It reminds me of the picture on the cover of this book in which a two-thousand-year-old couple whose flattened bodies were found in a bog in Holland seem to be walking convivially side by side and one of them has something like a thought, rising just above his head. They were found by bog cutters in 1904. A policeman was summoned and he rolled them together as you might a carpet and tied them on the back of his bicycle and took them back to town, where they ended up in a glass case in the local museum. Whenever I look at them I seem to be looking at me and my husband walking through a landscape, lost in conversation or in silence, our walk continuing in spite of time and the fact of death.

By now the sun is burning like a circle of flame as it moves closer to the horizon. We watch as a tight mass of grey-white birds with pointed wings swoop by with a rush of sound. Knots, which breed in the Arctic but come south during the winter months. Their many bodies are held in unison like a single body. They turn, and with the magic of their turning they vanish. They turn again and they reappear. They dance out across the rippled surface of the sea and they have gone.

The sky's colours are growing dark and thick and it's suddenly very cold. We are about to leave but stop when we hear a disembodied heralding cry that seems to erupt from a distant line of trees. The noise mixes with the soughing of the wind and almost could be the wind, but as it draws closer it disentangles itself and becomes a chorus of voices.

The geese fly low, directly above our heads. Wave upon wave of noisy warm-blooded creatures: the heaviness of them, the creak of their wings, the determined stretch of their necks as they make their way towards a place where they can be safe for the night.

On the following morning we get up at three thirty. We bundle ourselves into Jayne's car and drive for an hour or so until we reach a bird reserve on the edge of the bay of the Wash. It's still pitch dark and absurdly cold. I am wearing a coat, a jacket, a hat, two scarves, gloves and layer upon layer of T-shirts and jumpers and yet when I step out of the car the air cuts like a knife into my nostrils and fingertips and into a small patch around my middle which signals an untucked gap in one of the layers.

We are quite close to where the River Ouse used to flow into Doggerland. We are standing on one side of what was a sheltered estuary protected by the Dogger Hills. We are looking towards Dogger Island before it vanished.

This whole area has been built up out of the slow accretion of river sediment, so the flat muddy land and the shallow muddy sea merge into each other as if they were one and the same, but in the darkness before the dawn all that I can distinguish of my surroundings is what is revealed by the trickle of light from a little torch.

We find a path and follow it, not quite sure if this is the path we want. It is flanked on both sides by the looming presence of bushes and trees, some of which emit tentative fragments of song from the birds sheltered within them. I turn my torch towards a tree and something black tumbles out of it with a clatter of wings.

The path leads to wooden steps. We go up them and seem to be on some sort of man-made embankment. From this vantage point I can see a pink sliver of moon lying on its side in the dark sky. I can hear the lapping of water, but I have no idea what water it is. I am not even sure how far we are from the sea and how near to the shallows and mudflats of the estuary.

We walk on until we reach a wooden bird-hide and we go inside, glad for the relative warmth. By the light of my torch I read an account of the birds who come here during the winter months. Many of the pink-footed geese will have already migrated north, while the densely packed dawn crowds of knot only appear when the tide is high and so we will probably miss that spectacle. I tell myself it's better this way; if the conditions were perfect, then there would be the distraction of other people laden with binoculars and scopes and buzzing with talk.

We step outside again. There is a definite lifting of the light and I can hear the startled cries of birds; they sound as if they are surprised by the fact of the approach of a new day. I remember at school being asked to write an essay about how I could be sure the sun would rise in the morning and the question disturbed me because it was the first time I had paused to doubt the world's certainties.

Now I can distinguish the darkly shimmering surface of water to the east and something that looks like water to the west, but it's raised up and as bulky as a mattress; these must be the mudflats, exposed by the low tide.

More light and although there is still no orb of the sun, the breathing warmth of shades of pink and fiery orange are spreading out across the sky and clinging to the scatterings of cloud. In the distance, coming in from the land, I can see a smoky procession of white birds, flying just above the mud's surface. Every so often they explode into a flurry of upward flight so their whiteness is muted by the colours of the dawn and then they subside and return to their ordered lines. They keep on coming, purposeful and sure.

A different sort of movement is taking shape in the west. Again it is like smoke, but this smoke is dark as it rises up from the horizon. The geese have woken from where they were sleeping on the sea's surface and now they are flying in the direction of the dawn. I cannot hear them because they are too far away, but I watch their spidery lines criss-crossing the sky: sentences in a language I am unable to read.

We begin to make our way to the car. Just before we leave the edge of the estuary we come across a crowd of goldfinches. There are thirty of them at least, feeding on a wintry patch of teazel. The sound they make is like excited laughter.

I suddenly realise I have lost a blue and white spotted handkerchief that belonged to my husband. I wonder about turning back to look for it, but that would be absurd and so I leave it wherever it has fallen and I can see it there, long after I have left this place.

That was four months ago. Summer has come earlier than usual and the succession of days have been relentlessly hot and dry. The sky is milky blue and there are never any clouds to disturb it. The exhausted fields have faded into pale yellows and greys and the leaves on the trees make a rustling sound when a soft wind blows.

Yesterday I went swimming at Covehithe. There were quite a few people scattered along the beach, but once I was in the sea with the low outline of Holland invisible on the other side, it was as if there was no one else in all the world.

The wrinkled surface of the sea was covered with glistening clusters of white light that danced with the jostle of waves. Because I am an insecure swimmer I did not go out of my depth and every so often I stood my feet on the underwater land that lay beneath me. It was beautiful beyond words. I was only there for a little while and then I returned home.

Suffolk, July 2018

ACKNOWLEDGEMENTS

Jayne Ivimey had embarked on a series of paintings about Doggerland early in 2015. She shared the information she had so far gathered and we went on several wonderful research trips together along the Norfolk coast.

From conversations with Hugh Brody I began to pull closer to an understanding of the hunter-gatherer way of life. He very kindly read the book in its early and later stages, offering invaluable comments and advice.

Tim Holt-Wilson, with his knowledge of East Anglian geology and prehistory, arranged a number of walks to areas that still had traces of Doggerland.

Enrique Brinkmann, whose work has been part of my visual thinking for more than fifty years, generously provided the sequence of drawings that accompany the eighteen time songs.

Other friends I would like to thank are Tim Dee, Simon Read, Helena Simon, Simon Frazer and Sandra van Beek.

Among the many people who helped me with their knowledge and experience, I would particularly like to thank Robert Mutch, Ray Allen, Jonathan Stewart, Dawn Watson and Rob Spray.

A number of archaeologists and palaeontologists have accepted my lay-person's understanding with grace and good humour and have been very kind in sharing their expertise. I would like to thank Professor

Bryony Coles; Professor Martin Bell; Dr Jim Leary; Klaas Post; Dick Mol; Clive Finlayson, Director of the Gibraltar Museum; Nick Ashton, Senior Curator of the British Museum Palaeolithic Collections; Wijnand van der Sanden, Curator of Archaeology at Drents Museum; Professor Leendert Louwe Kooijmans, Professor of Prehistory at the University of Leiden until 2008; Pauline Asingh of the Moesgård Museum; Felix Riede of Aarhus University; and Ole Nielson, Director of the Silkeborg Museum.

My agent Victoria Hobbs has been an enthusiastic presence throughout the book's progress. Dan Frank, my editor at Pantheon Books in America, offered some invaluable advice at various stages of the work, and my friend Dan Franklin, who has been my editor at Jonathan Cape for the last twenty-eight years, understood what I was trying to do before I was sure if I did and followed the book step by patient step.

I have tried to give an accurate account of the huge sweeps of time I have been looking at. Any failures in presenting the information correctly are entirely my own.

The maps on pages 35, 85, 143, 165 and 183 are reproduced by permission of Bryony Coles. Maps devised by B.J. Coles and S.E. Rouillard. Copyright B.J. Coles and S.E. Rouillard.

INDEX

289